Death Letter
God, Sex, and War

David W. Peters

TACT16AL

Death Letter
Copyright © 2014 David W. Peters

First Edition

Because of the dynamic nature of the internet, any web address or links contained in this book may have changed since publication and may no longer be valid.

Brand names, trademarks, and service marks appearing in this book are the intellectual property of their respective owners.

The views expressed in this work are solely those of the author and do not necessarily reflect the views of the publisher, and the publisher hereby disclaims any responsibility for them.

Published by Tactical 16, LLC
Colorado Springs, CO

eISBN: 978-0-9898175-3-0
ISBN: 978-0-9898175-5-4 (hc)
ISBN: 978-0-9898175-4-7 (sc)

Printed in the United States of America

AUTHOR'S NOTE

Death Letter: God, Sex, and War is a nonfiction memoir of my experiences in war and my homecoming. *Death Letter* is written for combat veterans and those who love them. My fractured narrative contains explicit (definition: fully and clearly expressed; leaving nothing implied) scenes of my shattered existence during and after my deployment. I have substantially changed the names and identifying details of every person in the book for reasons of privacy and operational security. On February 20, 2014, the Department of Defense completed the public release security review of the manuscript. The opinions and characterizations in this book are those of the author, and do not necessarily represent official positions of the U.S. Army Chaplain Corps, the United States government, or The Episcopal Church.

CHAPTER 1
The Chaplain

Everyone writes one. At least, everyone who fights in a war does. Some of us seal it in an envelope and tape it on the door of our wall locker so our buddies can easily find it. When the First Sergeant, the senior enlisted man in the company, packs a dead Soldier's shit, he makes sure to weed out all the porn and anything else the wives or parents might not want to see. The folks back home receive a sanitized version of a man's wartime possessions. They also receive the death letter.

It's usually one page long and most are handwritten, although this war has also given us the email death letter. These are just as moving and contain fewer spelling errors. I wrote one of my first death letters on some Red Cross stationery when I first arrived in Iraq because I thought I was going to die in the first couple of days. Every explosion and rifle shot sounds so close and even though I am a chaplain and know that God is on our side, I know I'm not immune to the grim lottery of death.

I don't like the first letter. It's melodramatic and too short, so I tear it up. A few weeks later, I write another letter when I start traveling on more dangerous roads to visit the Soldiers in my battalion. My death letter is sealed in an envelope that says, "To be opened upon the unfortunate death of David W. Peters." It feels strange to write these words.

In my letter, I tell my two sons I love them. I instruct them to obey their mother and that I will see them again. The second paragraph is about my funeral. I don't want my father, who is a pastor, to preside at the funeral of a second dead son. The third paragraph is written to my wife, Anna. I tell her I love her and that it is OK for her to move on when she is ready. I sign it "Love, Dave."

My Mom, Dad, my now ex-wife Anna, and most of my friends call me "Dave." My sons always call me "Daddy," my lovers usually call me "David," but in Iraq, they call me "Chaplain." I love the brave men and women who call me "Chaplain." They know my voice in the dark. They know I'm with them. They know to get me when someone dies.

"Get the fucking chaplain!" The first time I hear someone say this I've been at Fort Hood, Texas on my first assignment for about four months. A dump truck rolled over a Soldier and he is pinned in the cab. The paramedics are saying the Soldier will die if they try to extract him. As I walk by the operations center of the unit, someone yells, "Get the fucking chaplain!" Later, when we are deployed to Iraq, the Soldiers often come and wake me first when we receive a message from the Red Cross. The Red Cross Message (RCM) is sent from home to notify us that a family member back in the States has died. They also wake me up when someone in our unit dies. When Soldiers see me coming in the witching hours of the night, they know someone is dead. News of death travels fast and everyone knows about all the deaths that take place during our deployment.

Sometime, somewhere in Iraq, I died.

A year after I returned from Iraq, I found the death letter I wrote during those first few days in Baghdad. I tear it up. It doesn't make sense anymore. I don't recognize the person who penned this letter or the God he wrote about. Even though his name is David W. Peters, he is dead. I'm not sure if the God that David W. Peters had on his side made it out alive, died, or just disappeared altogether. After I tear up my death letter into sad confetti, I begin to write another death letter addressed to the men and women who lost something in this war. For my brothers and sisters I will record the events that led to my death and the death of the God who was on our side in love and war.

CHAPTER 2
The Church

I fell in love with the church when I was a teenager. The particular group I was born into were Fundamentalist Protestants who took bold stands against premarital sex, drinking, and dancing. I want to serve her and lead her. I'm drawn to her power, and I sense her vulnerability in the world. I let her tell me what to do. So at nineteen, just as I'm about to leave for the United States Marine Corps (USMC) Boot Camp, I'm still a virgin and have never had a beer.

Two weeks before I graduate from my Christian high school and leave for USMC Boot Camp, a veteran stops me in the church lobby after a service. His name is Bill and he was in the Navy sometime after World War II. I know for certain that he didn't serve in the war. In a very serious tone, he begins to share with me about his time in the Navy. I can see the intensity in his eyes, and I hear a confidential hush in his voice. He tells me that I shouldn't join the military because the other Marines will take me to their lockers and show me magazines. He says the magazines will show me pictures of a woman's vagina. This is exactly what he tells me in the church lobby. I'm only nineteen, and I have never seen a woman's vagina in real life or in a magazine.

His face is full of concern and he scans mine for my reaction. He has a wild look in his eyes, and I wonder if he misses seeing those pictures. I'm too young to think anything is out of the ordinary. This is my first suspicion that God, sex, and war are somehow related.

I arrived at Parris Island, South Carolina, and I became a Marine. I march, do pushups, and sweat in the South Carolina sun for three months. When it's over I'm ready to kill and die. No one ever shows me a picture of a vagina.

I have come to Parris Island to become a man and my manhood is tested on a July day at the pugil stick course. A pugil stick is a big cue-tip that we use to simulate bayonet combat. We don football helmets and before we step into the sandpit Sgt. Hernandez grabs the helmet's cage with both hands and rattles our head around inside the helmet. He screams at us, "Let me see your war face!" He screams this and we scream back, "Yes, Sir" and we scream back at him. He rattles our heads inside our helmets until we give him a war face that beholds the proper degree of ferocity. Then we step into the sandpit to face the enemy from another platoon.

The first time I step into the ring I receive what the Marines call a horizontal butt stroke from my opponent's pugil stick. I reel and he stabs me with the bayonet end of the stick and the drill instructor blows the whistle and the battle is over. The second fight is a battle buddy fight. My partner, a skinny kid from North Carolina, and I are to drop into the sandpit two by two and fight as a team against another team of two from the other platoon. My partner trips on his run through the gauntlet and I jump into the pit alone with two attackers coming at me. I feel the three blows from their pugil sticks, the whistle blows, and I know I'm dead.

The third round gives me an advantage. Each combatant must run through a zigzag maze and then burst through a curtained door into the fighting room. I know my speed might save me. I beat my opponent to the pit and wait for him when he rushes through the curtain. He gets a butt-stroke and a bayonet jab and I am the victor. Sgt. Hernandez slaps me on the back of the helmet and I know I'll be proud of this moment when I'm an old man.

In Iraq, many years later, I wonder if I can conjure up my Marine Corps war face, and I wonder if it will do me any good. The face I learn in Iraq is blank to the suffering around me. I smile rarely and squint in the harsh light of the desert sun. I see the war faces on the Soldiers around me. They laugh and joke around their close friends, but when they're walking to their truck, carrying their heavy gear, they have the eyes of an old cop. Their eyes scan the area for death and danger. In Iraq, we're told we must know how we'll kill everyone around us. At any moment, the Iraqi army private who is asking for more fuel for his jeep will open fire with an AK-47. Be ready to kill everyone you are around, they say. I can tell the Soldiers are ready for this as they caress their weapons. The Soldiers look at all they see with blank faces and ancient eyes. The word "veteran" comes from the Latin, *vetus*, old. They have seen Valhalla and the burning boat that will bear them hence. Now I see the war face at the veterans hospital and the bars and I can see what they see.

During one of those steamy summer night on Parris Island, my worlds collide. I'm lying prone on a shelter-half tent in a sandy swamp. The lights from Hilton Head Island wink at us across the bay. My Boot Camp platoon, 1189, is in it's field exercise phase. We've been crawling through the muddy sand for two weeks. In the early morning, we march on the Tarmac that used to be the flight line during Vietnam. These runways witnessed thousands of young, skinny men flying off to Vietnam to face their enemy in the rainy jungle.

It's a hot night in the piney woods of Parris Island, and I'm lying next to my fellow Marine-to-be, Recruit Richard. He's from Texas and Richard makes sure to tell us that every time he gets a chance. Texans are supposed to become Marines in San Diego, but Richard's grandfather was a Parris Island Marine, so he requested the humidity of South Carolina over the dry heat of California. He's asleep and I'm using my red penlight to read a letter from Jenny, my high school sweetheart. Jenny wrote to me every day while I was in Boot Camp. I already read a bit of my New Testament. God first, Jenny second, although I look forward to reading Jenny's letter more than Paul's Epistle to the Galatians. In my excitement to read Jenny's letter, I forget the minor detail that recruits are not allowed to turn on lights in our shelter halves since we are under "light discipline."

I begin to read her words of tender strength. She is beautiful. I remember our embraces and arguments. I remember how she sat on my lap on the night before I left for Parris Island, the night of my high school graduation. I remember how she kissed and how she smelled that night. Nothing in my Marine Corps world smelled anything like her. This world was foul and damp. The smells of boot camp stay in my memory like the smells of war and I will never be free of them, or her.

Jenny is my equal and I love and hate that equality at the same time. I read her words and suddenly I feel a presence. It's Sgt. Hernandez. I find out months later, at the obstacle course, that he has seven children with his wife. He and his wife are the same height. I also discover later that he's an administrative clerk. He handles personnel actions in his real life, but here, in the bizarre world of boot camp he's the man who makes all eighty of us do footlocker dips until we collapse. He's the one who calls us all "Yoo-hoo." "Hey, Yoo-hoo!" "Get over here." He's the one who tells us we're no good. He yells that we're all pussies. He's the man from whom we want to earn respect.

The presence of Sgt. Hernandez is so real that I freeze. The human animal has several options when faced with danger. He can flee, fight, or freeze. I can neither flee my platoon nor can I fight Sgt. Hernandez. All I can do is freeze. He looks down at me with my love letter and my red light. He says two words, "Eat it, Yoo-hoo." He follows this command with silence.

So I begin. I tear the top of the letter off and stuff it in my dry mouth. I chew it, lying on my stomach in the shelter half. I chew and chew until some saliva helps me swallow it. I stuff the rest of the first page into my mouth. This is the only page I've read. I chew it and Sgt. Hernandez watches. Occasionally, he looks around, scanning the area. He's looking for more romantics, like me, who forgo sleep to read love letters from high school sweethearts who will never bear them children or endure years of loneliness for the sake of war.

I eat the second page with more enthusiasm for I am now embracing the sacred order of the Marine Corps. We don't need to read love letters because we can eat them. The girls will love us whether we read the letters or not. I only want one person to love me, and he's wearing sergeant stripes.

After the letter is inside me, I can now feel my New Testament in my jacket. We are all sleeping fully dressed and we've been sweating in the sand all day. As I hear Richard snoring next to me, I know my calling. I know this romance with Jenny, God, and War will go on forever, for I've been seduced by all three.

Washington, D.C.: After Redeployment

Today I'm an Army hospital chaplain in Washington, D.C. I'm sitting with a Soldier who is talking to me about the people he killed in Iraq. He describes a car full of kids that kept getting close to the convoy. He knew they weren't going to blow him up, but he shot them just because he could. He looks at me and says, "They broke the rules. They would have broken them again." He says he isn't worried about Judgment Day, even though he killed them for the wrong reason. He knows it's over now. What he *is* worried about are all the women in heaven and a few in hell that will speak against him on Judgment Day. He knows the women will tell God what he's really like.

While he continues to talk, I'm thinking about a woman. She has long dark hair and is the mother of my children. I am scared of her. I, like my Soldiers, fear nothing, except women. We can't disagree with their accusations. I can only hope that on that day, when I stand before God, there will be a line-up of women who will say I treated them right, even if it didn't last forever. When I'm one with the Universe, I hope their voices outweigh the voice of the only woman who knows the truth.

CHAPTER 3
Anna

Baghdad, Iraq: Three Weeks into the Deployment

I'm at an Army Forward Operating Base (FOB) in Baghdad, Iraq. I've been here for three weeks, and I'm lying on the floor listening to the rockets roar over my little shed. The little wooden building shakes like a cheap apartment beside the train tracks. The floor of the office is dusty but I don't notice the dust until the moment that I realize I'm trying to burrow deeper into the floor. If a rocket hits near the building, I want to be low enough to avoid the shrapnel. I know that if I'm standing when the rocket hits nearby, a jagged piece of steel could sail over the concrete barrier outside my office and rip through my neck. One more rocket roars over the office, and then all I hear is the whirring of the fan and the beating of my own heart. I never knew war could be so full of contradictions—so full of things that just do not belong together.

I can feel my heartbeat against the thin wood of the office floor. I've heard rockets before, but this time they whizz right over the little shed. War is loud. The explosions and bombs are so loud that I feel the sound waves hitting me in the chest and my ears ring for hours. I always wear earplugs with the hope I'll have some hearing left when I rotate back to Texas. I sometimes wished there were other ways to dampen the impact of war on my senses.

I signed up to be an Army chaplain shortly after the invasion of Iraq. I was working as an assistant youth pastor in a suburban church before I joined. I was too young to be a father figure to the aging congregation. At best, I reminded them of their kids, at worst, their grandkids. In the Army, I'm a venerable old man. I think I joined at the age of 27 for the hollow prestige of being older than everyone else. My first counseling case was a young Soldier who was caught looking at kiddie porn on his roommate's computer. The guy is only sorry he got caught. Yes, this is different from what I dealt with in the church before I left for the war.

After just a few months of being a chaplain, I know about death. I see old people die in the hospital. I now know how the face changes when a man, even a very old man on a ventilator, breathes his last breath. I see some fight it to the very end, their eyes wide with fear and pain. I'm silent when the nurses increase the dosages of morphine until the living heart stops beating.

I'm called to the hospital to bless a stillborn baby. The baby is tiny and is presented to me in a pink basket. It looks like an Easter basket, and I imagine the plastic green grass surrounding the baby. The baby is wrapped in a blanket and the mother is sitting in her bed staring into space. The mother has already seen the baby. The nurse leaves and the three of us are left. The dead baby is more of a presence than her mother or me. I take the basket in my arms and cradle it. I pray for the baby, a lamb of Jesus' flock, and I pray for her mother. I hold the basket for an eternity.

The nurse calls me a few days later and asks me to do the funeral. The nurse is not sure if the father will show up. I preside over the funeral. The mother is there but she is silent. The father didn't come; he is in Iraq, on a deployment. The tiny pink casket stays closed for the entire service.

At 27 years of age, I have closed the eyes of the dead with my own hands. Chaplains nurture the living, care for the wounded, and honor the dead. If anyone is dying, their job is to get the fucking chaplain.

Baghdad, Iraq: Three Months into the Deployment

"Get the chaplain," I hear someone say. They must know I'm near for they didn't drop the "F" bomb. I don't have a problem with it being said this way. The Army is a simple operation. When something happens, leaders must decide which asset to push into the fight. When the situation is ambiguous, be it a screaming wife at battalion headquarters or the death of a child, a chaplain is the obvious choice. I like the ambiguity of my calling. I embrace it.

I hear them call me as I'm walking through the battalion headquarters during my first few months in Iraq. An Explosive Formed Penetrator (EFP) has ripped its way through a Humvee. Two Soldiers are dead and two more are at the hospital. The Soldiers are from my sister battalion. Their chaplain is making a beeline for the hospital with the unit's commander to see the wounded. Good leaders know to show up. When legs and arms are ripped off by an explosion on a spring afternoon, that's all anyone can do.

The Executive Officer (XO), the second in command, from my sister battalion wants a chaplain there to receive the rest of the unit as they come back from their mission. This unit's mission is called Route Clearance. They drive down the roads of Baghdad and her suburbs looking for roadside bombs or, in military language, Improvised Explosive Devices (IEDs). When I first heard this, I wondered if there were ways of blowing people up that aren't improvised. On this hot day two men, two husbands, two fathers, two Soldiers, two lives of improvisation are now over. They are in the most certain category of humanity—death.

I don't run over to where the platoon parked their vehicles. Death will hang around and wait for my arrival. Their trucks are huge and have V-shaped hulls. They were invented in South Africa to keep white men alive. These vehicles are supposed to be bombproof. However, the EFP is new and it can blow a hole in a tank. The more armor the U.S. Army welds to the sides of our vehicles, the bigger the bombs become. Dr. Seuss was right about butter battles after all.

When I step out of the 110 degree sunshine and into a dark room of the plywood building, the temperature inside is at least 120 degrees. It's like an oven and the 12 to 15 guys in the unit have their jackets off and sit on folding chairs in a circle. Their armor is sitting in a pile in front of each of their feet. Dark spatters of blood are on most of their pants and one man's pant leg is soaked in blood from his knee to the boot. This is a Soldier's blood that was shed within the hour. It's dry, because blood dries fast in the Iraqi sun.

I sit down and keep my jacket on. I know the unit's First Sergeant will be there shortly and order the bereaved to put their jackets on. Discipline and safety are his responsibility no matter who lives or dies. Sure enough, the First Sergeant ducks through the low doorway and surveys the men in the folding chairs. He tells them to put their jackets on. Most of the Soldiers scowl and slowly put their arms into the sleeves of their sweat-soaked uniforms.

The First Sergeant sits down, and I introduce myself as the battalion chaplain from the engineers next door. I explain that their chaplain is on his way to the hospital in the international zone to see the wounded Soldiers before they fly to Germany. From there they will fly to their mothers, fathers, wives, and children at Walter Reed Medical Center. I tell him about the ground rules for what we're about to do. The first rule is that anyone who wasn't in the attack needs to leave the room. Two sergeants who man the radios in the operations center get up and leave. The men who remained in the room were at the scene when the road erupted. The second rule is that everyone must speak for themselves and say what they think. I make it clear this is not an investigation nor is it a formal inquiry. I then turn to the Platoon Sergeant and ask him if he can describe what happened.

The Platoon Sergeant begins the story by describing the patrol route they do in the early morning. They were on a side street that ran parallel to Route Michigan. The Platoon Sergeant says, "We were coming south under this bridge, and the fuckers had an EFP or something huge behind the bridge abutment. The blast hit and rolled the lead vehicle. The convoy stopped and I was in the back of the vehicle. I had my driver race up to the burning Humvee. It was on its side. I jumped out and Smith and Gomez were already trying to pry the door open with a crowbar. The doors were blown off on the passenger's side and were buried in the sand."

The Platoon Sergeant pauses and stares at the floor. Sgt. Gomez takes up the narrative and says, "I was trying to pry him out, man. It was so hot next to the vehicle." Sgt. Gomez stops. I ask, "Who were you trying to pry out?" Sgt. Gomez looks around the room and says nothing. Then he goes on, "I couldn't do shit." The Platoon Sergeant who started the story is talking again but in a different voice. It's detached and matter-of-fact. It's the voice of a man so overcome with emotion that he has no emotion. He finishes the story of how they extracted the living and the dead. I listen and don't say a word. One by one, all the Soldiers speak the dead men's names. One man in the room says he should have been in the lead vehicle but was switched out minutes before the mission.

Then Specialist Smith, a 19-year-old white kid from Ohio, says one of the dead guys, Evans, always wanted him to come visit his family in Arizona. Evans had tried to lure him there with a picture of his sister. Smith says she looked like she was fourteen and he shakes his head and says, "No way in hell." Then he pauses and says, "Of course she *was* hot." Everyone laughs. Sgt. Gomez shakes his head at the floor and says, "*Sheet*, man." I hear the words "shit" and "man" and feel that those are the only two words that make sense in this war.

In spite of the blank stares of the men, none of them can yet grasp the finality of their friends' deaths. It might take years for that to happen. Until then, I will carry their stories. I will carry them and never tell anyone. I will put each story into a little jar and place it on a shelf in my basement. The jars will not touch one another. Then I'll turn my back, shut off the lights, and go upstairs.

I carry my own stories but they aren't that sensational. There aren't any scenes of me pulling the wounded out of a burning truck while the bullets pop around me. All I remember is the endless nights of driving around Baghdad in a convoy of Humvees. I remember staring out the window with my helmet leaning against the metal door. My helmet is so heavy after I wear it for hours. I wait for the sound of the blast that will kill me. It never comes. I remember wondering what I will feel right before the blast. I wonder if I will see God. I have a dream where I'm blown up. I see God and he looks like Bob Dylan but his voice is different.

It's night now and the convoy stops at a worksite where my engineers are building a guard shack for the Iraqi Army. They work at night since the curfew keeps the streets clear of Iraqis. I struggle to open the door of the up-armored Humvee and then I swing my legs out. I slide out of the tan vehicle and stand up. The armor is heavy and it's 2:00 a.m. I walk around the worksite, shake hands, and try to cheer up the men and women who will stay up all night clearing dirt and garbage off the side of the road. I go see them at night because they are tired, bored, and covered in the shadows of war. I want them to know that I'm one of them, even though they know I'm different. I walk around Baghdad without a rifle and with a cross on my chest. They know I didn't have to come see them at night. I come at 2:00 a.m. because I love them.

They clear the garbage and dirt so insurgents can't hide bombs. It's important work but it's still garbage relocation. I can see the deep connection between each of them as they work together on these projects. They know that if they die, they will perish together, so their bond is strong. The deepest relationships I will ever experience are forged here in this war.

After a night of driving around Baghdad, my convoy rolls back to the base. The up-armored Humvees sound tired as their diesel engines rattle over the potholes of the Baghdad streets. Everyone but me will clear their weapons in the clearing barrels filled with sand so they don't take a loaded weapon back into their barracks. Chaplains can carry weapons according to the Geneva Convention, but we decided against it a while back. The bombs go off ahead of us and behind us, but there's never a direct hit on my truck.

Sometimes before a mission, the Soldiers say they're glad I'm going with them because now they will be all right. I tell them the founder of my religion was killed about 500 miles from here, and I don't expect my life to be any different. They all laugh. Sometimes I think leaders should give the troops more hope, even if it's a false hope. But the Soldiers understand why I say this. They know the crazy calculus of death can't be written in chalk on the blackboard. It can't be written in a book in ink. It can't be carved on the wall of a stone church. Shit happens. Death happens. Love happens. That is all we hope for in the hot Iraqi night.

The evening is hot, and I'm sweating. Now that I've been in Iraq for several months I'm used to being soaked all day. I walk to the Kilo Company Headquarters building because I heard that one of their Soldiers had shot someone. I sit down with the twenty-something sergeant who tells me that he was in a guard tower and someone shot at them. He says he shot back and the Quick Reaction Force (QRF) drove out to the building and found the dead body of the shooter. The sergeant shares that everyone was patting him on the back and saying what a good shot it was. It was a good shot, I think. I wish that I had done something heroic and brave like the sergeant. But then the sergeant   begins to cry. He says he thinks he crossed a line. He killed someone and everyone told him it was OK to kill that man who shot at the guard shack. But this sergeant knows in his human heart that he will never be the same again.

He killed a man and that man's life and death are connected to him in the most intimate way two humans can connect on the face of this planet. Something in me knows he's crossed a line, too. I want to tell him he was just doing his job. But I know this won't work. The sergeant has fear in his eyes. Perhaps it's the same look the young Iraqi shooter had when he felt the surprise of a bullet in his windpipe like a bee sting. Perhaps he had the same look in his eyes when he lay on the dirty floor of the abandoned concrete building. Perhaps his eyes watched the pool of his own blood grow larger and larger on the floor just inches from his face. The sergeant wants to tell the shooter he's sorry he had to shoot him. I say that maybe one day he can.

When Soldiers can't inflict wounds on the enemy, they inflict them on themselves. It's hot and it's now 3:00 a.m. A convoy's about to roll out, and I'm walking down the line of trucks to pray with my Soldiers. A young sergeant engages me in conversation. He tells me about a new knife he just bought. He pulls it out of his sheath and holds it in front of his chest. Since he is wearing a heavy vest with ammo pouches, he has mounted the 10-inch knife on his chest, with the point facing up. He shows me the knife and sheaths it near his opposite shoulder. His eyes lock with mine and he says, "Chaplain, I'm going to be fine." I look at the knife and it's not in his sheath. He's stabbed it into his shoulder. The blade of the knife has pierced the cloth of his jacket and dark red blood is starting to blotch on his bulletproof vest. He's managed to drive the knife into the only vulnerable place on his upper body, his armpit. He looks me in the eye and tells me he'll be fine. Then he slowly collapses to the ground. Instantly, I'm calling the medic who is in the rear vehicle. The medic says the knife's point has touched the bone of his shoulder and he can't go on the convoy. I walk to the first aid station where he gets bandaged up. He's ashamed and humiliated by his self-inflicted wound. Later, when I return home I begin to realize that all the wounds of war are self-inflicted.

A few days later, a Soldier knocks at the door of my quarters. It's 2:00 a.m. and I don't think it unusual. He works on the night shift, so one would expect him to find his chaplain during his work hours. After all, I told the Soldiers on the night shift that they can come to talk with me anytime.

He comes back a few days later at the same time, and I'm too tired to talk. I ask him what is going on and he spins out a few stories about the assholes he works with and for. I know there's something he wants to tell me, but I'm too tired to ferret it out of him. I say good night and I sleep until my alarm summons me to a meeting with a company commander at the gym. We work out together and I feel like the workouts keep me sane.

Four weeks later, the sergeant goes on leave. He flies back to Texas and picks up his car from his apartment's parking lot. He drives the car to the police station. He tells the police he's been having sex with his girlfriend's teenaged daughter. The police put him in jail. Now I know why he came to me in the witching hours of the night. If only I had the energy to ask him why he came that first or second time.

Soldiers are superstitious and they all carry at least one charm to ward off their own death. They carry handkerchiefs with the words from Psalm 91 printed on them. There's an Internet myth circulating about a unit in World War II that prayed this same psalm and not one of their men died. Someone printed the psalm on camouflage bandanas and handed them out by the thousands. At first they were desert camo, then they switched to the Army Combat Uniform (ACU) pattern. This pattern is a gray and white checkered pattern and it's meant to camouflage us in the desert, or in a gray, urban environment. For a while, during the transition, we wear a mix of camouflage, desert and ACU. We can tell how long a unit has been in Iraq by the camo pattern. This is the secret knowledge of combat.

We fold the Psalm 91 bandanas in quarters and place them in our helmets, on top of the pictures of our trucks or lovers. Maybe the psalm will protect our heads from death or a traumatic brain injury. Maybe they'll just absorb our blood.

Psalm 91 says "a thousand shall fall at thy side, and ten thousand at thy right hand" but it won't kill you. Because the people in the psalm trust in the Lord, they won't die suddenly and unaware. Psalm 91 says "thou shalt tread upon the lion and adder," and no harm shall come to you.

The devil quotes this same psalm to Jesus in Matthew 4 when he tempts Jesus. In this story, the devil takes Jesus up on the highest part of the temple and dares him to jump. The devil says that if he jumps, the angels will catch him in their arms. The devil supports his claim by quoting Psalm 91. The devil says that if Jesus jumps the angels will "Bear him up in their arms, lest you dash your foot against a stone." The devil dares Jesus to be a daredevil. But Jesus doesn't jump. He just stands there and tells the devil to shut up. A few years later when Jesus hangs on the cross, God turns his face away from his bleeding son. He cries out, "My God, My God, why have you forsaken me?" No one comes to his rescue. A thousand stand on that day in Jerusalem, watching him die slowly. Only one man falls and not one angel comes to save him.

Before a night mission, we gather in a circle and talk through the route and the objective. We go over contingency plans and rollover procedures. We make sure the radios work and that everyone has a map and plenty of ammo.

When the precombat checks are over, most of the team lights cigarettes in the darkness. The low growl of diesel engines fills the night and the headlights of our trucks cast their beams through the cloud of cigarette smoke.

In these moments, I see the holy incense going up before an ancient altar made of uncut gravel. The warriors invoke the god of the road, the god of love, and the god of war to favor them over the enemy in the unlucky lottery of death. The incense goes up and then I say my prayer. I pray that we will all have courage for this mission. I pray that those we love would be safe at home. I thank God for our lives. I thank God that this war came to us, on our watch, so our children and grandchildren can have the fruits of peace and security. We walk to the vehicles. Our boots crunch through the rough gravel and we squeeze our armored bodies into our vehicles and roll out.

Iraq is like Las Vegas. It's hot, and the dining facility stays open all night. Everything in Iraq runs 24/7 and there are few clocks. The twisted jackpot is death and nobody beats the house. The unlucky winner is a dentist one day and an infantryman the next. It could even be chaplain. As I stand in the circle of warriors night after night, I whisper into the darkness, "Burn your incense. Call on your gods. We can use all the help we can get."

I write to my wife Anna and call her every day. When I'm in the backseat of a Humvee rolling down a Baghdad street I think of her. She is the happy place I go when I can't stand the heat, the exhaustion, or the boredom. Every day when I kneel down to pray in my room, I think of the ways I have not been a good husband to her. I think of my failures big and small. When I return, I'll buy her the minivan she has been saying we needed for three years. She has the most thankless job of war. It's her responsibility to tell the world how I'm doing when they call her. I know we will emerge from this war with a passion for one another that will be worthy of the World War II couples that are memorialized forever for their long-distance relationships.

I call her when I come in from a mission and I'm exhausted. She is just going to bed and the sun is coming up in my war world. She tells me about the boys and how her friends are cooking dinner together. I miss her. I ache for her. We call several times a week, but we rarely laugh together. The work we must do on the phone is too serious. There's always the shadow of death creeping into the edges of the phone call.

After a vehicle is blown up, medics, engineers, and carpenters drive out and clean up the blast site. They walk around slowly scanning the ground for the fingers, hands, or anything they can put in a plastic bag. They pick up the remains and put them in special bags. They look for clothing and dog tags. They tow the damaged vehicle back to the base to a restricted area where all the blown up vehicles await transport to Kuwait. In this high-walled parking lot, they scrub out the inside of the blood-and-explosive-stained vehicle with powerful cleaning compounds. They hose away the blood and bits and pieces of the men and women who died in the twisted, burnt steel. The medics do this with great joy. They are not happy they are called to the scene of death, but they are happy they can endure it, and their special gifts are of some use in this world.

My medics enjoy their exclusive priesthood at the altar of blood and death. They have passed the initiation of seeing and smelling dead blood and flesh. They will carry these images and smells with them until they turn 40 or 50 years old and can't fall asleep at night anymore. They can't sleep because they see the images they've filed away in the back folders of their mind. They will not be able to avoid the blank stares of the dead or the severed hand that still has a wedding ring on its finger.

The Soldiers who are called to clean up a blast always find the helmets and the boots. There's usually little left of the boots but burnt leather and rubber. The helmets have bits of hair on the inside with sticky blood. The recovery team takes the helmets and boots and makes a display in the front of the chapel for the memorial ceremony. They take a rifle, fix a bayonet to its muzzle, and stick the barrel down in a wooden stand. On the butt of the rifle they perch the helmet. In front of the rifle, they place the empty boots, heels together, in the position of attention. This is the symbol of a dead warrior. Somewhere between a man's helmet and boots he has marked his brief, 23-year-old passage on this planet. He was only part of this world for a moment, and that moment was one of war.

I went into the religion business so I could understand death. I wanted to see life and death and I wanted to do something about it. I went to college and then to theological seminary where I learned to translate Greek, Hebrew, and Aramaic into English. I also learned about theology and stocked up on an impressive set of conclusions and beliefs. I wasn't ready for what I would face in war. I didn't know there would be so much death and I would see most of it with my own eyes and touch it with my hands. In the valley of the shadow of death there are only metaphors and mysteries. Some clergy could tap into this unseen world and I wanted to be one of the ones who could. What if I could pull back the curtain and see the metaphysical universe behind it? When the war started, I knew exactly where I needed to go. In a few months, I was in Baghdad and my wife and sons were thousands of miles away. I survived. That is the only way Soldiers remember war.

When I return from Iraq, I tell as many stories as I can to anyone who will listen. I'm never finished talking about it. I do this for about three weeks until I realize no one gets the point of what I want to say. So I stop telling the stories. The only story that makes sense to people is the one about the time I piss in my helmet.

This story happens while I'm visiting some Soldiers on a Forward Operating Base (FOB) on the other side of Baghdad. We drive past the squalid neighborhoods of East Baghdad. There are burning cars and young men with dark eyes staring at us as they stand on the side of the road. When we arrive at the FOB, they tell a major in the Tactical Operations Center (TOC) about the route we traveled and the major says, "Christ Almighty!" We're lucky to be alive since that road was black. A "black" road means no one's allowed to drive on it. In the previous week, they lost several vehicles on that same road. I stop by the chapel and visited a Chaplain named Reggie. He offers me some Gatorade. Reggie takes the powdered packets and pours them into a cold water bottle—shake and serve.

It's about 11:00 p.m. but it's a hot night. I gulp down the whole bottle of Gatorade fast. When the convoy is almost ready to roll out, I have to piss, so I decide to go around to the other side of a dump truck. It's dark and I'm wearing body armor with a large bulletproof groin protector hanging off the front. I'm also holding my helmet in my hand so all I can do is unbutton my fly by feel. I pee and something sounds strange. In the dark I'm pissing directly into my helmet which I can't see. Now it's full of my own urine. I dump it out on the ground and try not to get it on my boots. At that moment I hear my Chaplain Assistant yell for me to get back into the Humvee because the convoy is rolling out. I say, "Shit!" and take my canteen and dump the water from the canteen into the helmet. I swish it around, dump it out, and put it on my head. I fasten the chinstrap so no one confuses me with John Wayne. It smells like Gatorade and berry-scented piss. This is the only story that makes any sense to anyone.

When I stop telling stories, another story takes its form.

Fort Hood, Texas: After Redeployment

This story starts just days after my unit arrives home from Iraq. My unit flies home in a huge commercial passenger jet. Shortly after takeoff, the heater breaks. The temperature in the cabin drops to about 45 degrees and we don our warmest clothing and sit and sleep. The pilot offers to land the plane and make repairs. We say, "Fly on. We have women waiting for us."

I've been back in Texas for three months now. I'm looking at the phone bill and notice my wife is calling the neighbor and talking for hours at a time. He's a Major, one rank above me, and a good neighbor. Almost every day after work he and I throw a Frisbee or a football while our kids play in our front yards. I "go long" and he throws a high spiral and I catch it on the run. I turn to him and we both laugh. It feels good to catch a ball on the run.

He talks to my wife for 123 minutes on Valentine's Day that year. I can't remember a time when I've been on the phone with her that long. The calls come from pay phones all over town. Soon there's only one number calling and that's the Major's cell phone number. It's as if they want to be caught.

Denial serves me well for a few hours until my friend, Rich, confirms my suspicions. He takes one look at the phone bill and says she's cheating on me and she's been doing so for some time. I go to the Army's lawyers. They tell me to either confront the man or tell him to stop, or I will be accused of being an accessory after the fact. So I call the Major on my wife's phone and tell him to meet me at the Whataburger, a fast food burger chain. We meet. I ask him to stop having a relationship with my wife and he nods his assent. I can't tell him, or order him, to stop having a relationship with my wife. I've never ordered a higher ranking officer to stop anything. I'm scared to hear an order come out of my own mouth. I tell him that I think he lacks integrity, and he mumbles the word "Integrity" back to me. He looks at the orange Whataburger table and shakes his head. What the boyfriend doesn't understand is that I'm not angry, I'm only terrified— terrified of the loss of my family, my credibility, and my life. My wife doesn't matter much. All I care about is my fragile ego and I can feel it slipping away.

My wife has been jumpy for weeks. She's always looking over her shoulder, even when she has her back to the wall. Since I came home from Iraq, this all seems normal. I'm just happy to have running water from a faucet and the ability to pee naked in the middle of the night. A year without running water and indoor plumbing make a man grateful in ways that defy reason and sense. I also discover my new obsession of pairing Port wine and computer games. I sip, I play the game, and I feel nothing.

I discover that my wife is obsessed with the neighbor, who is a father of four and the husband of one minivan-driving woman. My wife and I used to look out the window and laugh together about how the neighbor's wife pulls into their driveway with speed and force. The intimacy of laughter is all we had. I say, "She's coming in hot!" We both laugh again.

My wife and this neighbor have chemistry. They are soul mates with a future, and they are fucking like rabbits. Later, as the smoke from the infidelity bomb clears, I remember seeing my wife going out to get things like paper towels and coming back with her hair in a different arrangement. Of course, she's the kind of woman to always have the paper towels and I think nothing of it at all. I'm happy to have more time to escape the sense of dread and death I carried in my duffel bag home from war.

I walk down the street past the houses of my Army neighbors to confront her at the park under a blazing Texas sun. I see her on the park bench talking to her boyfriend on her phone. I hear a rushing wind sound in my ears. It's like the roar of a train. There's a brooding presence in the air and no one is acting normally. I'm not seeing reality anymore. A man across the street is mowing his lawn in a suit and tie. A child is walking on the sidewalk with a cane. A cat is chasing a dog down the street. I walk up to her without any words to say, "What's going on? Are you cheating on me?" These questions are the best I can do.

I only started investigating her when she finally refused to have sex with me. She refused after cheating on me for three months. She brings her new iPod to our bed and kept it on while we made love with all the indifferent passion of a six-year marriage. I don't mind that she keeps the headphones on. I only mind when she says it hurts.

She says it feels like I'm raping her. I feel weird and dirty, like I'm doing something wrong. She follows by saying she doesn't want to do it anymore. "Anymore?" I ask. She says, "Never again," and looks away.

So the next day I see an expert—a man who has a degree in marital and family therapy. The expert says I should read some books, become a real man, write her some love letters, and win her back. I read the books and think they're naive and hardly intellectual. I write two cards and leave them in her minivan. That's when I see the phone bills and confront her in the park. The phone bills don't lie or protect me from the truth. I know she's with him, and I beg her for an explanation other than that she is in love with the neighbor. I ask if they have some sort of teacher-student relationship. She just laughs. Then fear comes on her face when she sees the look on mine. She knows that I might kill her. She knows that my emotions are about to awaken and I will not be safe. She knows that I will not be a reasonable professional who understands that all relationships end and this affair is for the best. The look she sees in my eyes is somewhere between madman and frightened child.

Before I left for Iraq and even after I returned, I wasn't scared she might fuck the neighbor. I like the neighbor and I'm certain my wife is not the kind of woman who will ever cheat on me. But she did, and the rushing wind in my ears is coming from somewhere. She will not give in. She will not grovel and beg for forgiveness. In a few days, she's on a plane for her parent's house.

I'm not sure what to do so I drag myself to work during the day and wander the streets and parking lots at night. My stomach fills with a sickening nausea and I lose about thirty pounds because I no longer want to eat. I lose so much weight I could go on TV as a spokesperson for a weight-loss product, but only I know it came at the price of heartbreak. I never knew heartache is physical until I feel it in my chest.

My chest hurts every day for four weeks. I can't explain why it's the most painful at 5:30 a.m. and 9:00 p.m. It hurts so bad I rarely eat. When I do eat, it's at Whataburger. That place seems to house the last scrap of my self-confidence, because I can look my rival in the eye in a grease-stained booth. This is the only thing I'm proud of anymore.

I call my wife every day and she talks to me. She talks because she's afraid I will report her boyfriend to my Commander and an investigation will be launched. Adultery is still a felony in the Army, and my neighbor could lose big if the affair was discovered. I listen, I accuse, and then she hangs up because it's late. It's always late and now I know it. In all the post-adultery fights, I only call her a whore once.

In the days after she leaves for her parents' house, I'm staring out the window and I wonder if she'll come back. I wander into the empty room recently vacated by my young sons and smell the sheets. They smell like home and love. They're the only antidote to the smell of war. Movies, books, and stories can't completely capture war or love because they can't capture the smells. It's night, and everything is as she left it. She's the same but somehow I'm different. I weep. I pace.

At night I walk the hot suburban streets of Texas and watch the bugs swarm all around the giant light posts. I stare at the cracked sidewalks with bits of grass poking through them. I listen to the sound of the interstate in the distance. I walk the streets wishing a car full of guys will stop and pick a fight, or I hope that some woman will tell me to get in, take me to her apartment to fuck. I will be happy with either alternative. Neither happens. I stumble home and then stumble to work for another eight or nine hours of this masquerade until I retreat into the painful reminders of this empty house.

The movers come and I watch them pack up the baby blankets and the disassembled crib. The house is even emptier now. I drive north to Pennsylvania where my sons and their mother are holed up in the basement of her parents' home. I drive straight through the night and play with my ring as my left arm hangs out of the window of the minivan. One time it almost falls off. I think I might kill myself if I lose the wedding ring.

I stop at a fast food restaurant where the cashier looks at me with hungry eyes. I look back at her and know she wants me. I've been driven to her by the night, and she wants a man who is of the road. She looks at her co-workers as if she's in charge. She is. She looks at me and for a moment I believe she's in charge of me. Something in this moment gives me hope that maybe, just maybe, there is a woman who wants me. But tonight, I'm going north to save my family, to win my wife back from her temporary madness. This thought helps me take my burger and its special sauce and walk away.

I drive north and show up at my wife's parents' house afraid and angry. Fear and anger pulse through me in equal parts. Most days I can't tell the difference. Her parents are uncomfortable and she is even more so. She keeps looking over her shoulder and I tell her how much I love her and want her back. I say this in front of her parents but it isn't that convincing. I tell them that every time I went on a convoy in Iraq, I took my ring off and put it on my open prayer book. I tell them how I'd kneel by my bed and pray a Psalm in the hope I'd see the ring and the book again. If I lost my arm or life I didn't want to lose the ring. I tell them this and she rolls her eyes. She suffered in the war, too, but my stories always trump hers. I'm melodramatic, but for a good reason. Everything I do is the right thing for the wrong reason. I know this, but I can't stop.

I take my boys to my parents' house in Pennsylvania for three weeks while I try to fix my marriage. This isn't what I wanted to do on my leave but this is the Soldier's life. The boys' clothes are neatly folded in a big suitcase. Every morning I wake up and put my sons in the jogging stroller and roll down the bike path along the creek. They snack and I run. I push them up the hills and we just cruise for six, then eight, then twelve miles. I'm rarely tired these days.

I became a runner the day I found out about my wife's affair. It's the only way I can deal with the pain and rejection. I run because I hate men and there are many men running on the road. I run behind them and overtake them. When I pass them, I steal their soul. I imagine turning around, seeing them veer off the side of the trail, and crumple in the ditch. With their soul I am strong. They fall, one after the other, as I run faster and angrier.

He and I had been training for a marathon together, just a few weeks before I found out about the affair. He's the better runner, having ran a marathon or two already. I want to learn how to do it. When we run we share how difficult it is to come home from a war. He tells me about the chaplain in his old unit who broke his leg playing soccer in a pick-up game. After a long-distance run one Saturday morning he tells me he must have pulled something and can't train for the marathon anymore. Later, I realize he's saying he doesn't want to spend three hours alone with me on Saturday mornings while he's fucking my wife.

A few nights after I arrive at my parent's house, she calls me and tells me she wants to meet. We meet in a smoky diner in Red Hill, at 9:30 p.m., halfway between her parents' house and mine. She says she doesn't want a divorce. I keep my cool and say, "Oh, really?" She never looks me in the eye but tells me she wants to stay married. Her boyfriend has broken up with her over the phone and she wants to stay married now. I wait for her to say she loves me but she never does. I ask her if she loves me and she says that she's so far away right now. I don't understand. I am happy but there's a nagging sensation that she's just resigning herself to a lifetime of drudgery with me. So it has been and so it ever shall be.

I ask her if she's interested in counseling. I'm ready to start making love to her right here in the smoky diner even if there is a table between us. I want her in a way that is primal and possessive. She is worlds away and although my heart tells me this is true, something deeper tells me otherwise.

I learn that I'm a mammal when I find out my wife is cheating on me. The feelings that rush through my body leave me wasted and weak, but I'm feeling them for the first time. I've lived over 30 years and never felt anything until now. I find out I'm just like the lion that goes crazy when one of his females is impregnated by a young rival. Of course, in my wife's case, her lover is at least 10 years older than her and has had a vasectomy. The fact that he's at least two inches shorter than her troubles me, too, but I put that out of my mind. I remember a young Soldier once saying that we are all the same height lying down. I'm not sure how much lying down has gone on but I have my suspicions—especially when she infers they did "it" as much as they possibly could.

I tell this to my friend, Rich, as we drive in my wife's minivan. He sniffs, looks around, and says that it does smell like sex in here. A wave of fear and panic hit me even while I know it's funny. Everything that was once funny can now send me reeling. I panic at the slightest memory of my failures in the marriage. Every time I hear a husband talk down to his wife, it makes me sick, for I remember that tone too well.

In spite of several failed counseling sessions in three different states, my wife files for divorce and shall hereafter be known as my "ex." There is a certain fondness in the term "ex." It's cute, short, and precise. It defines someone by that which she is not. It even rhymes with sex, which is what this was all about in the first place.

CHAPTER 4
Shannon

Washington, D.C.: After Redeployment

And so I enter the world of singleness with one quest—I want to get laid. Just like I steal the souls of the men as I pass them on the trail so I will steal the souls of women. I will show them that I have power and that I can break their hearts. I will love them but never trust them. I will get what I want, and they will pay for that transaction. I survived divorce with most of my money and unlimited access to my sons. My self-confidence, however, has taken a beating. My ex-wife once compared my lovemaking skills to that of her lover and I can't forget that. I know she was right and now I'm hell-bent to change that.

As the judge was signing the divorce decree, I begin a new assignment at an Army hospital in Washington, D.C. There I give spiritual care to the Soldiers and Marines who were wounded in Iraq and Afghanistan. I also get a call from an official in my church.

Reverend Evans calls me at work and says the Credentials Committee wants to meet with me at their next meeting. I'll be one of the items of business. They've already sent me a letter stating I'll lose my ordination and endorsement as a chaplain because I'm now divorced. The rules are clear. A minister can't be divorced. It's the unforgiveable sin. Reverend Evans asks me if October 30 is OK for me to attend. I say, "Yes." October 30 is my birthday.

After thirty, all birthdays are tinged with the fast approach of death, and the celebrations die down a bit. So it feels appropriate for me to be standing before the Credentials Committee on such a day as this. I'm wearing my Class A uniform with its shiny buttons and war ribbons. I wait in the lobby of the church the Committee is using for their meeting. I small talk about the Army with a janitor who served, and now has a son at Fort Campbell. I become a chaplain to this man and listen to his story. In the other room they're taking it all away. But, for this moment, I'm still a chaplain and I will carry their stories. That is what I do. Get the fucking chaplain—he'll carry your story. I listen to the janitor until a

27

committee member summons me to enter the room.

They tell me they're sorry about all this and ask me to recount what happened. They offer to bring the matter up in front of the Annual Conference so there can be a law change just for chaplains. I clearly tell them I don't want any special treatment. If the rule is changed, it shouldn't just be for my circumstances. I don't tell them what my wife has done. They'll have to listen to the gossip for those details. I look around the room and know firsthand how my Soldiers, and all Soldiers from all the wars in the history of the world, must feel when they come back to their hometown. No one understands us. No one knows what we have done, or what was done to us. No one knows me.

Soon enough I'm picked up by a nondenominational organization for such a time as this. They ordain me after I fill out a written application, and I'm back in the religion business. I'm a little embarrassed about my quick ordination, but fathers can't be too proud when there are child support payments due.

The greatest compliment I've ever received is that I'm a good chaplain. I love the work and I love the men and women in the Army. I love the poetry that can flow in a good sermon. I love the reassurances of forgiveness. I even love the funerals where every ear, Christian or otherwise unaffiliated, hangs on my every word. Most of the time this is all I love.

I'm going on dates, mostly from eHarmony, but I'm afraid of commitment. I know this is typical and cliché, but I don't want to be married anytime soon. I know if I marry someone soon, I'll cheat on her later. I don't want to cheat. I miss my ex like crazy, but there's a craziness growing inside me every day. I know I want to be with a woman. I dream she'll make the declaration that I'm a man and that I'm desirable. That's all I want from women. The affair makes me question my manhood and my attractiveness. No one wants me and I have no one to protect or shield. What is a man if he knows not his time or cannot kill for those he loves? As Steinbeck or someone said, "A man that will not kill for his woman is worth nothing at all."

I answer an ad on Craigslist. She's looking for a real guy and I send her an email. She writes back. We exchange pictures and I think she is hot and young. She thinks the same about me. I tell her my age and she tells me I'm fuckable. She tells me she has a stripper pole in her Dad's workout room where she lives. She says, "It's a good workout," and I ask her to share more. I tell her I'm an Army chaplain and I'm not sure what's right or wrong since I've been divorced. I drop off my kids with their mom and we meet on a Sunday night, at a restaurant equidistant from each other. We sit across from each other and sip from small mugs of Coors Light. As the beer dwindles in the cup, I ask if she wants to come over to my apartment. She says, "Sure" and follows me in her sensible Toyota. We step inside my apartment, and sit down on the couch. I ask her about the stripper pole and if she could demonstrate. She says she can with her shirt off.

The window blinds are not peep proof, so we move to the bedroom of my two-room apartment. On the bed we kiss in silence. I can't believe I'm with a woman. She's the first woman since my ex-wife, and I remember our divorce sex. It was passionate and passionless at the same time. It was angry sex and it worked. It was silent. I had sex with my soon-to-be ex-wife at her parent's house shortly after I learned of her affair. This was three days after she told me she didn't want a divorce. After the sex, we just put our clothes on and left the room. All I said was "Thank you." She said nothing. We were strangers now and our sex proved it. Perhaps she was preparing me for dating sex.

This woman I'm kissing now is 23 and I'm 33. I whisper in her ear that I want to make love to her and then I ask her, "If we have sex right now, what will we do tomorrow?" She says matter-of-factly, "We'll have sex tomorrow." I see a pattern emerge and it feels a lot like marriage. Now, I can only think of tomorrow and the future. After we do this, I don't ever want to see her again. I want to tell her I feel trapped. I feel like I'm Odysseus, she's Circe, and she will trap me on her island. I know I'll try to leave, in spite of its abundant pleasures. I roll on my back and stare at the ceiling. I prop myself up on an elbow and look into her eyes. "I can't do this," I say. She says, "Damn, this always happens."

I start to put on my shorts, but she has somehow dressed herself already. She turns and walks out the bedroom door, "You only wanted to fuck me because I was black." She is black but that wasn't the reason. I wanted to fuck her because she looks a lot like my ex-wife who isn't black but resembles this woman in an uncanny way. I don't tell her that. I just look sheepish and say, "I'm sorry."

I walk her to her car in front of my building. She turns and says she going to call the hospital tomorrow and tell my boss what his chaplains are up to after hours. She says, "Are you the kind of person that's taking care of our wounded Soldiers?" All I can say is that I never lied to her. She looks away, then she looks at me and tells me she has a secret. She says she just got divorced, like, a couple of months ago. I ask her why she didn't tell me that. She said she didn't think I'd like her if she was divorced. Then she gets mad again. For a moment I think she might appreciate me quitting before we had sex rather than after we did the deed. She doesn't appreciate this nuance.

After she leaves, the fear sets in. It rolls in through my open window on the night air. I lie on my bed and stare at the ceiling. My chest hurts. What if my boss knows I met a woman on Craigslist and got her naked in my apartment? What if my ex-wife finds out? What if God finds out? I show up for work the next day. I call a priest friend and confess my sin, but I'm not sure it's a sin. My friend reassures me that, in my defense, I didn't have sex. If I'm called on the carpet for my sexual indiscretion, I could always claim this. Refusing to have sex with a woman can be noble. She never calls my boss. A few times that day I think all the black women are glaring at me, but then I realize this is all in my head.

Work is tough these days. I have to constantly meet new people and try to get them to like me. I want them to think they have a good chaplain. I want them to think that I don't have any problems. My boss threatens in staff meetings to fire all the chaplains if we mess up. I envision about fifteen different ways I can accomplish this. I'm waiting for the other shoe to drop, and I'm sure it'll be a high-heeled shoe. But I Soldier on. I make my visits to the wounded Soldiers in the hospital. When I'm overwhelmed, I go into the bathroom and lock the door and stare at the mirror. I talk to my reflection and hope that I am heard. On these days, this is the closest I ever get to prayer.

In the empty hospital chapel I try to pray. I pray that I can be the kind of man my ex-wife could love and respect. I pray for forgiveness for never caring about her in the way that made sense to her. I don't pray she'll change her mind but that I can change mine. I ask, like St. Augustine, that God will give me chastity, but not yet.

I'm getting better at picking up women. I sip beer at a bar and look at the world around me with disinterest. I take out my cell phone and pretend I have a call. I do a couple of fake laughs so the women who are checking me out as-sume I have friends. Women are so relational they trust anyone who has as many relationships as they do.

I get a look on my face like I'm about to leave, and then I turn to the woman and say something. The words come from the part of my brain that fears, fights, and fucks. It always fails to get their interest. But I have her interest because I'm the only man that is making a move on her. She answers a text message on her phone from a man too cowardly to call. I wait. Then I ask her about her friend. "What friend?" she says. I say, "The guy who just texted you." She tells me about this guy and all the problems between them. She says she worked it all out in her head and in long conversations with girlfriends. She's never spoken about these problems with the guy. She's only here in the bar by herself to get back at him. I ask more questions about the guy, and he starts to look shabbier by the minute. She talks and I listen. I listen like there is no tomorrow. I listen like my life depends on it because tonight it does. I smile at her. She notices my dimples. I dare her. It doesn't matter what I dare her to do. She feels the growing risk and begins to like me.

When this happens, I get ready to leave and ask her if she wants to go. We walk out of the bar. When the cold air hits us, I remember what I want to be-come and all the conversations with the mirror come back. I think of my ex-wife sleeping in her big bed alone, and how I'm the last person on earth she would want to be next to tonight. I turn to the woman whose face has a glow from the neon Miller Light sign. I tell her to take care. I ask, "Will you be alright getting home?" She says she lives across the street. I tell her that I'll walk her home. I walk her to the doorway of her apartment building and look deep into her eyes. I tell her she is amazing but I need to get home. She gets it. I jog home to my apartment. I think of the moment when she would have done anything for me even though I didn't care. In every one-night-stand there is a longing for love, or grace, or something in-between.

I'm not ashamed of the fact I see a counselor. I need someone who can show me this grace that only a therapist can give. I go to therapists like a wine taster goes to Napa. I evaluate their bouquet. I think about their provenance. I savor their words. I find one I see weekly and she asks me about my love life.

I tell her I have a woman that could be a girlfriend except for my commitment issues. The counselors always take my side and so I never trust them.

Although I don't trust them, I do listen to them. They are all emphatic and encourage me to explore my sexuality with these women. I tell them I want to have sex with a woman and they always approve. In fact, this is their main point of unity—sex should never be inhibited. This is the only thing I can hear after a while.

Canada: Three Weeks before September 11, 2001

The thing that haunts me most these days is my impotence. Yes, it's true I have produced offspring with my ex-wife, but that took years to perfect. Our wedding night was a disaster. If we hadn't been in Canada, we might have annulled the whole thing. We were staying in a bed and breakfast on our first night together. I laid my wife of five hours on the bed and took her clothes off. We've never been naked together until this moment. We are both fundamentalist Christians and don't believe in premarital sex, at least I didn't. On our first night together, I lose my erection when I try to put a condom on for the first time. There is nothing to give at this point. I panic. This doesn't help things at all. She remains calm and stoic. She doesn't get mad. Does the infection start here, deep in her soul, in this moment? Does it grow over the years and manifest in her affair with a married man? I know this is where it starts, because when I ask her why she cheated, she says, "It was because of what happened on our wedding night."

On the wedding night I put on my clothes and drive to Taco Bell. I bring back some burritos, or tacos, or whatever the hell they are, and we eat them on our wedding bed. I think to myself, "Tomorrow will be different." But it isn't. It's just like the wedding day. Nothing happens and now I'm scared. I have no desire for her. I like her and we are friends. We need each other, but we don't want each other. On our fifth night together I finally enter her. It's a bad combination all around—the rubbers, the naked woman, and the lack of intimacy. It's too much for me and I know, after our divorce, that one of the lessons of the affair is to learn about my own sexuality. When I was sure she was cheating on me,

I knew she was right. She had been right all along. She always did the wrong thing, but for the right reason.

CHAPTER 5
Camille

Washington, D.C.: After Redeployment

The truth was the Grand Alliance—the elusive agreement between my head, heart, and cock—had not happened. In my mind, these three things, added together and working in harmony equal love. Unfortunately, I've yet to experience this. I know it all has to come together or it will not end well. The woman I'm seeing now is smart, successful, and divorced. She is perfect in every way. I never refer to her as my girlfriend, even though we share a bed every third weekend. I try to make love to her but I don't want her. I don't have sexual feelings for her so I can't get it up. I claim I'm not ready for the commitment of sex. The Grand Alliance is not complete, and my body will not ignore this. I like this woman and I see a future, but it's only because it's safe, secure, and will result in economic stability. My penis thinks otherwise.

One morning in my apartment as I reach for her, my penis fails me again. Instantly I flashback to my honeymoon, Taco Bell, and the shame that made me want to scream. I couldn't scream then because my new wife might have been horrified, and rightfully so. Yes, it's my honeymoon all over again and I can't bear it. I feel like I'm a 25-year-old virgin again. I've undressed my bride and all my desire is gone. I waited until marriage for sex and now God has played the cruelest joke on me of all. I gave God my teenage sex life and he took it away for good. I'm a failure at sex, the one thing that every Tom, Dick, and Harry does with such mindless enthusiasm. So much so, the world is populated with unruly, unwashed children. The easy stuff is always hard for me.

I think I need chemical help so I make an appointment with a psychologist who encourages me to explore my sexuality. I tell her that I'm coming up short. I say I think I'd like to try pills for ED, and she agrees to refer me to someone who can give me a prescription. I meet with a doctor my own age and fight back embarrassment. I feel like a loser for needing help with my lovemaking. I'm a single chaplain, and I hope he won't judge me. The pharmacist gives me a

90-day supply of tiny, tan pills and a list of possible, severe side effects, which include blindness. There are about 30 pills in the amber pill bottle. I go home, take half a pill, and wait. Nothing happens. I feel a little tingling around my eye sockets and think I might be going blind. The blindness doesn't scare me as much as the necessary explanations I'd have to make at the ER. I wait, and realize that although the pills give me the confidence I sorely need, the problem with sex is mainly between my ears. My head, heart, and cock must align. I can't ignore the Grand Alliance.

When I was 8 years old, I visited a museum that was full of little votive gods and goddesses from the Iron Age. All the little gods are about four inches high with six-inch penises rising straight up in front of them. I remember being so disturbed by this I asked my mother to hold my hand while I covered my eyes with the other hand. I walked through the rest of the museum this way. Yes, penises have scared me for too long now. Something must change and I must press forward.

Washington, D.C.: After Redeployment

The workday is done, and I'm at the bar. It's crowded with well-dressed, older men and women from the bank administration building across the street. An Asian woman sits down on the stool next to me and orders an Amstel Light. She's in her mid-forties and hot in a way that only older women can be. She's bent over her cell phone and texting like a teenager who is riding in a car with his parents. She's dressed in a tight gray dress with high heels that dangle from the bar stool as if they have a mind of their own. I turn to her and ask if she knows why her beer is named Amstel. She glances up and gives me a once-over. She looks back at the phone and says, "No." She thinks I'm a nerd and I am. I say, "It's the name of the river that flows through Amsterdam. It's a Dutch beer." She looks away. I stare at the bottles of liquor behind the bar. They're lit from below with purple and blue lights. They're beautiful and remind me that their shape speaks of what is inside.

I ask her who she's texting and she tells me it's a guy. I ask if it's her boyfriend. She says, "No, he's just a friend." "Well," she says, "a friend who likes to have sex with me. He is a math teacher from Pennsylvania. He's remodeling a house and can't come down this weekend." I ask her how often he comes down. She says they see each other about every ten days.

Then she turns to me and says they met at a bar in Dewey Beach, in Delaware, and spent the weekend together. She says its why they call it "Do me Beach." He's a musician. She told him that if he played her a song she would take off her clothes for him. I said, "Wow, did you?" She says, "Yes, but he wasn't that good of a singer." She's separated from her soon-to-be ex-husband and she explains she would be divorced already if only the state of Maryland would grant the petition in less than two years. My mind plays with the idea that she is married for a moment, and then I consider her to be emphatically single. The high-heeled shoes help me reach that conclusion. I listen and she tells me about the men in her life. She brags about how they come to her apartment and have sex. After sex, she goes to her bed to sleep by herself. She says she always sleeps by herself. She doesn't need to be held. I ask about her husband and she tells me she was a good wife for years. She only stayed in the marriage for her 16-year-old son.

Then she looks at me and says she has a lesbian friend and they've had sex a few times. She stresses that she isn't a lesbian but wanted to give it a try. She says she needed to be loved and so she let the lesbian friend do it for her. I sit on the barstool in silence and wait for her to go on. The math teacher from the beach keeps asking her to arrange a threesome, but her lesbian friend won't go for it. I think she only speaks of the lesbian friend because it's a sure way to get a man sexually aroused. It's working. I know she likes the sexual power she feels when a man wants her.

I walk her back to her car in the garage and she gives me a ride back to my apartment. She has a convertible Lexus and I think about what it would be like if we cruised in the summer with the top down. But tonight it's cold. When she stops the car in front of my apartment, it feels like she's a friend's Mom and she's dropping me off after a birthday party. She leans over and I kiss her. Her lips are full and they melt into mine. I can tell she wants me by the way her lips relax and open. I feel her leg and go higher. I pull back and look her in the eye. "Give me your phone number," I say. She does and I get out of the car and I don't thank her for the ride. She tells me to call her and I say, "OK."

I walk into my empty apartment with an eye for any changes. I look at the shoe rack to see if there are any differences from the way I arranged them when I last left. I know I can't trust this woman in the Lexus so I pour some red wine into a white insulated cup. I swish it around in my mouth and spit it into the sink. I stare into the sink and go to bed. As I lie there, I'm happy a woman wanted to make out with me, but I'm sad the woman of my obsession is somewhere up north in another world that doesn't include me. I think she might be just like this woman, telling stories of a ménage a trois for men who want her. I know she cheated on me for the same reason this woman cheated on her husband. She didn't know any better. She was in love. These are reasons enough for a woman. Is it true that a woman in love has no morals?

It's a week before I call her. I'm out running in the city and feel the urge to connect with someone who thinks of me sexually. She answers and asks if I could come over and play her some songs. I arrive at her apartment at 7:30 p.m. She's wearing sweat pants and a sweatshirt. I look into her son's room and she leads me to the couch. I play her a song that I wrote for a female company commander I served with in the Army. It's slow and I put my heart into it. I close my eyes and sing. At the final line, I look right at her and sing, "If you go out to see the sunset/you'll always walk back in the dark." I pause and look down at my guitar. She looks at me and says, "That was amazing."

She moves closer to me on the couch and I kiss her. I look into her eyes again and ask about her other boyfriends. She says one of them came last night to watch the football game. She says they sat on this couch and watched the game. Then they fucked and he started drinking beer until he passed out. In the morning, he wanted to make love to her. He called for her to come into bed with him. He showed her his erection, and she just rolled her eyes and went to work. I look at her and say, "Camille, you deserve better." I tell her that all these guys just want to have sex with her. She needs to grow as a person so, in five years, she can say that this time in her life was good for her soul. I tell her that's what I want to do. I want to look back in five years and not have any big regrets. I don't always want to be like this. I don't want to be in the ragged club of the broken. She looks into the distance and suddenly becomes a girl. She becomes a girl who looks at me and tells me how her parents are immigrants from the Philippines. She likes how I cut the Chinese take-out with a fork rather than a knife, since Filipinos never use knives. I leave and drive home. I don't like to drive but since I went to see about a girl it's okay. I drive home and wonder what it would be like to have sex with a woman who wants me. I know what it's like with a woman who doesn't.

Camille invites me to an after-work happy hour at the same bar where we first met. She's in the tightest red dress that makes all the men stare as if there is no shame in the universe. I sit at the bar and she grinds her hips against my leg even while she hugs a newly arrived coworker. I've never seen someone go to this much effort to turn me on. She wants me, her divorce is signed, and I'm ready.

I'm dressed like an adult in real pants, without cargo pockets, and a sweater. Unlike the rest of the guys at the bar, I had to go home, take my uniform off, only to put on clothes that look like work clothes. She drives me to my apartment, and we make out as I fumble for the key to open the door. I have one ED pill in my pocket but I don't take it. I don't need it tonight. She has a six pack of Guinness. She brings me a bottle, but I just sip it. Not even my favorite beer is going to interfere with what I'm about to do. We undress each other, I feel myself enter her, and it's the most natural thing in the world for me. She loves it. She begs for it. I'm so happy when I finish I almost weep. I gasp "Oh, my God." This is the only time I've ever said this for anything. After I make love to her, I hug her. I cling to her as if she is the last scrap of a life preserver after the shipwreck. She is.

I sit next to her on the couch and she looks into my eyes. I don't want a relationship and she has assured me she doesn't want one either. After two years, her divorce is final, but I see a look in her eyes. In her eyes I see a small bit of her soul and I pull back. I think she loves me. She loves me in some weird, sexually maternal way. I don't want to share life with her but she wants me to share it with her. I know I'll let her down. What happens now? Will she go crazy? Can she read my mind and see I despise her for being so easy? I say it's late and she ought to be going.

I see her one last time when she brings me a Christmas present. She even brings presents for my sons, even though she's never met them. This is too much for me. I thank her and she drives off. The presents for the kids push me over the edge. I call her later and apologize that I'm not going to see her again. I say I can only think of myself, and that's a deal breaker for me. She's sad but says she saw it coming. There are advantages to having sex with older women. I can only love them because they know I will leave them and they will understand.

CHAPTER 6
Amy

Washington, D.C.: After Redeployment

I break up with the woman to whom I never refer to as my girlfriend. We've been dating for five months. I met Amy on eHarmony and she's an attorney in Delaware. I call her and let her know this is the end. I tell her I haven't been faithful. She says she's going to throw up and hangs up the phone. I wait and stare at the phone feeling like shit. Why do things have to go this way? Why do I always have to make the tough decisions? Why does my experiment with love have to hurt another human being who is full of light and life?

Maybe we could make this work but I know we can't. She calls back and asks me what this means for the future. I pause and say it means we will never talk again. There's silence on the other end of the phone. Then she takes a deep breath and gives me the most eloquent, simple speech about how she thinks this could work. She says she believes in me, but she understood this is how it goes. I couldn't believe she could be so complimentary after how I ended it. This was the best speech I've ever heard. It's a moment of grace in an endless age of law and karma.

After our first date at a bar in Wilmington called The Dutch Masters, she loans me her copy of Bono's autobiography. Bono, the lead singer of the band U2, says that law and karma are true. What we abuse comes back to abuse us. We break the law, and the law breaks us. But then, without invitation, grace breaks through. The grace of God overwhelms the law and karma. She's an amazing woman, but I'm not an amazing man. I'm a man obsessed with my ex, still hoping for the day when she will call and say she wants to be married to me again. I'm a man on a mission to hurt someone as bad as I've been hurt. I'm doing everything in my power to protect my fragile psyche and it's working. It's like I'm immune to heartache. But I'm enjoying this immunity too much. No one can hurt me like my wife hurt me. This is one thing I can be sure of in this uncertain world. I have paradise in my reach, but it is a feckless heaven. It's all empty without her.

Baghdad, Iraq: Six Months after Deployment

Men serving in times of war can't live without women. In Iraq, we all call our women as much as we can. We wake them up at 3:00 a.m. just so we can hear their voices, even if it's a morning voice. Every morning in the Battle Update Briefing (BUB), the voice of a young female lieutenant updates the Division Commander and all the subordinate commanders. It's a classified briefing and most of it's devoted to telling the bad news from each sector of Baghdad. I remember the morning report of how many vans of dead bodies were found the night before. Ten or fifteen dead bodies were left in an abandoned van. The bodies belong to young men who were abducted and killed in the rapidly escalating civil war that just started in Baghdad. In 2006, we aren't allowed to call it a civil war. Civil war would imply we created a situation that is complicated. Instead of a civil war, we focus on how Iran is meddling by making bombs that kill our Soldiers. We can't yet say the people we've helped for three years are starting to grow weary of our presence. I imagine fifteen bodies lying in the back of the van, fully clothed, stacked like luggage.

The voice of the young female lieutenant is beautiful. She's like a DJ on a radio station. I imagine her to be young, beautiful, and wearing a short Army haircut. Every morning I wait for her to report on the sector that contains the neighborhood or *muhallah* known as the Belladias. I drink the word in like wine. I don't know why I like to hear her say it but I look forward to hearing it every day. I hope she says it again in the briefing and she often does. When she moves on to another sector, I'm sad she won't say it anymore. This is the truth about men, and war.

One day at the BUB, there's a different voice conducting the briefing. It's a man's voice. Two weeks later she comes back. As she begins her briefing, she pauses for a moment, the General breaks in, and his disembodied voice says *they* missed her voice and *they* are glad she is back. He didn't say *he* missed her, but he did. He spoke for all of us men who had called up Mars, the god of war, and didn't know that Aphrodite, the goddess of love, would show up and we would all forever be seduced.

As far as I know, American Soldiers don't rape many Iraqi women. However, on occasion, they do sexually assault their fellow female Soldiers. They also fall in love with each other and find ways to hook-up in the hot sheds of the base. I fell in love with several women during that year, but I never spoke of it. It's part of the job of a chaplain to get emotionally involved with women. But we never cross the line of touch or sex. Married Soldiers find lovers, and the single ones pair up quickly. My female Chaplain Assistant is hit on almost every time she goes to the Post Exchange (PX) to buy soap or whatever. Her suitors leave love notes for her in my Humvee. She just rolls her eyes and I wonder if she subconsciously knows they're all feeling the throbbing pulse of Mars and Aphrodite in their young bodies.

When I'm in Iraq, I visit the Troop Medical Clinic (TMC) on the base. I'm there on certain afternoons when I feel like getting away from my unit. I always see some of my Soldiers waiting on appointments for their coughs, rashes, and back injuries. We chat and I try to encourage them with what encouragement I have left after eight months in Baghdad. I hang out in the break room of the TMC and soon become friends with a young Army doctor from somewhere in Maine who runs the place. During the rainy season, when the roads turn to thick mud and everyone curses the land of Iraq, the doctor and I go out to eat. Our wet boots grow heavy in the thick mud. When we arrive at the Dining Facility (DFAC), the floor is covered in mud and cardboard to protect the tile floor.

At dinner, the doctor leans in and looks me in the eye. He says I can't tell anyone this. I agree, knowing he's probably told a dozen people already. The doc says a guy came into the clinic last night from the MP brigade with a lollipop stuck in his ass. I say, "No way!" The doc says he was wearing his physical training shorts and the stick was sticking out of the shorts like a tail. "What kind of lollipop?" I ask. "It was a round lollipop, flat and round, the kind with the swirls," he explains. I think about how long the guy must have spent trying to pull it out himself. I think about who was with him when it got stuck. I think about the point at which the guy decided to go to the TMC. The patient said he accidentally sat down on the lollipop and it got stuck. I suppose this is sin. All I know is that we are all sinners, and sin is just looking for love in all the wrong places.

CHAPTER 7
Eva

Washington, D.C.: After Redeployment

After the divorce, I drive up to my ex-wife's apartment to pick up the boys. They are wearing jeans and sweaters, and I adjust the rearview mirror so I can look at them while I drive. My oldest son asks me, "Why is Mom is so mad at you all the time?" I ask him, "Are you sad we aren't together right now?" He says he's sad and that he doesn't like living in two houses. I tell them I don't like it either, but that's the way it is.

I put them to bed in my apartment. They ask for a monster story, and I ask them which monster story they want. They want to hear about Medusa. So I tell them the story and they hang on every word. I say how Perseus used his mirrored shield to look at Medusa. They get excited as I tell them more about how her mythical powers would turn him into stone if he looked directly into her eyes. The boys love mirrors and the Gorgon's snaky hair, so the story is perfect. We kneel and recite the "Our Father", and I sing them a song I wrote for my oldest son's fifth birthday. He likes his song and asks me to play it again. I play it one more time, and I kiss them both. Their soft cheeks are divine. They say I have cactus cheeks and that mommy doesn't. I tell them this is a good thing and shut the door. I remember my own dad kissing me goodnight and thinking the same thing.

On the balcony of the apartment, I look out into the night. Cars drive by on the road below. Each one is headed somewhere. Only the parked cars lack a destination. Like Abram in the Old Testament, I look up at the sky and question the God who promised me a good marriage. I tell him I had damn near done everything I was supposed to do and now everything is a fucking mess. My voice rises from the whisper of my mind and I speak. I yell at the Master of the Universe and tell him I didn't like what happened. I taunt him for how he turned his Almighty back on me when I needed him most. I rail on, "Don't you care that she left me? Don't you want us together?" There is nothing but silence. I know that answer, but I can't believe it. I know that God loves my ex-wife as much as he loves me. I feel most betrayed by this thought. Whose side is God on in a war? Whose side is he on in a divorce? Whose side is he on in the Super Bowl?

Then the questions break. I whimper, sob, then burst into a full-on ugly cry. I weep at the silent stars and the fingernail-shaped moon. I hope all the clocks will stop and die with my soul. When I stop weeping, I hear a voice. The voice is silence. It is the stillness of the unconditioned. It is a voice unconditioned, like a horse standing still. There is Kierkegaard's royal coachman seated above him with a whip, poised to strike at the slightest movement of the horse. It is the Universe or God or the Ground of Being herself that has a message for me. The voice says, "You can leave her now." The voice is not my own. My weeping has been heard, but God has surprised me in the worst way imaginable. I don't believe him and walk back inside.

I think about the story of Jacob in the book of Genesis on the shores of the Jabbok Creek wrestling with a man. The man is strong, but Jacob doesn't give up. He puts the man in an armlock and puts his knee into the man's side. The man can't move. Jacob pins him there for almost an hour and the man begs to be let go. Jacob says, "I won't let you go until you bless me." Jacob waits for the blessing of the wrestler as the prenautical twilight begins to lighten the sky. Faces are now becoming distinguishable. Now is the time when armies attack. The wrestler does not bless him, but with a sorcerer's magic, he shrinks Jacob's leg muscle and he howls in pain. Jacob lets the man go. He lies on the ground and holds his leg with both hands. The man walks away.

Jacob rises in pain. He looks down the path to where the man disappeared. He begins to follow and realizes that his leg still hurts. He can only limp. Jacob remembers with satisfaction that he pinned the man down until he pulled this trick on him. Jacob limps home and the blessing is his hurt leg. I know how Jacob feels. I wrestle with this man every night, and I can barely walk in the morning.

God doesn't care about Jacob's conflict with his brother. God doesn't care that Jacob has two wives and eleven children who might die when the sun comes up. God only cares about one thing—winning the wrestling match. God tests Jacob's resolve just as he's about to lose everything. I realize this is the only challenge in the universe. God loves the world and the humans that make it spin. God loves the stories we live out, unaware we are on the great stage of the Almighty. When I wrestle God on the banks of my own Jabbock Creek, I know he is an old god and he doesn't care about my marriage. God doesn't care about my war. He only cares about me. Of all the revelations in the universe, this one truth shocks everyone who hears it.

The next evening, I'm in a supermarket wandering the aisles. I put some things in my cart I think might impress a sophisticated city girl. I stop in the wine aisle and look down the twenty meters of wine. I stand in front of what I call the "Odd Bottle" section. I glance at the bottles of Port, Sherry, Vermouth, and Manischewitz. There's even a small bottle of plum wine waiting respectfully for a successful Japanese man. I know this is my section. I spot a well-dressed couple, a breeding pair, in matching black wool coats compare bottles of Sauvignon Blanc for a party. They would never come down to where I stand. I'm like these bottles. I take a bottle of Manischewitz off the shelf and open it. I take a drink and look over at the couple. They look back at me in a mix of shock and pity. I take another drink and slowly push the cart towards the register, pausing only long enough to put a bag of pita bread in the cart.

Even though I've been back from Iraq for over two years, I'm still there. I'm alive there, dead here. I'm myself there. I'm scared there. Over there, there's always a golden day before me when I will see my family again. Now there's nothing hopeful on the horizon. There's no magic day where all manner of things will be well. It's just an endless succession of seconds that will one day stop.

Israel: After Redeployment

I wonder why I'm fascinated with the Middle East while I'm flying to Tel Aviv on an El Al flight. It's a big plane and most of the passengers are Israeli. They're quiet and I watch them out of the corner of my eye. I can only hope that going to Israel will help me process some of my feelings about this troubled part of the world. The last time I flew across the Atlantic I was on my way to war.

On the night I flew to Iraq, I said goodbye to my wife and my young sons. Then the buses come and all the Soldiers in my battalion climb aboard.

The buses drive through the night while brand-new cars pass us. The interiors of the SUVs are lit with the glow of DVD screens. I wonder if anyone in the SUVs know we were going to war. At this moment, I know I'm alone. I know no one will care that I've been to war. Perhaps it will be an interesting fact that might last a few minutes in their mind.

But for now, I'm off to Israel to travel to the Holy Land without an entourage of Soldiers who glare into the night and protect me. I'm alone and now I prefer it this way. There are no expectations here. I think about whether I'll spend more time in Tel Aviv or Jerusalem when I see a flash of flight attendant. She turns to answer a question from a man in a seat behind her. She turns like a dancer and I'm transfixed. It's a violent turn full of slow passion and confidence. I take a sip of red wine and watch. The man mumbles a question in Hebrew and she responds with one word, *Shalosh*. She says it with such intensity that, for a moment, I can't breathe. *Shalosh*. It was a word that forms a connection in my brain that will not easily take its leave. She turns and glides up the aisle. I've never seen anything like it, and I want to see more.

I get up around the eighth hour of the flight and wander back to the galley to use the bathroom. She stands there and offers me coffee. I say, *"Shukran,"* then realize that although she speaks Arabic, she is Israeli and prefers to speak Hebrew. I ask her if she likes her job. She says, "It's okay, but I want to be a physician." I ask her what kind of physician she wants to be, and she says that she is interested in oncology. I ask her for her number. She looks at me and says, "My number is 1707, Washington, D.C. to Tel Aviv, Tel Aviv to D.C." I thank her and wait for her to leave. She turns softly with a bit of hesitation. I think it may be desire that slows the pivot of her hips.

I buy three miniature bottles of whiskey from another flight attendant who looks like he enjoys these kinds of transactions. I polish off all three bottles. I don't see the hot flight attendant because I'm asleep when the plane lands. The plane is empty when I wake up, and there's a vacuum cleaner running somewhere in the back. I grab my backpack and head out into the terminal.

There are about a hundred taxis lined up outside the terminal, waiting in the hot Israeli night. Every taxi is white and every driver is the same shade of brown. At first, I'm sure my driver is an Arab and this bothers me. I can see myself in a homemade video, sitting in a chair with black flags with Arabic script waving behind me. Five men with scarves wrapped around their faces stand behind me with AK-47s. One of them takes a knife and begins to cut my neck from my left ear to my right ear. He lets go of my hair and steps back. My head falls back like a PEZ dispenser and hangs there for a second. My bones break, my skin rips, and my head falls behind me to the floor. I can see him cutting. I can feel myself falling, but that's all I feel.

I know they're just like me, the Arabs, but I can't trust them yet, ever since my year in Baghdad. I saw what they did to their own too many times. We discovered minivans full of dead young Iraqis during my year serving in the war. The young men were pulled from their cars at makeshift checkpoints all over the city. Then they execute them. They put the bodies in the vans our Soldiers in the morning. They report the number of dead men and full vans to the general. I know they'd sell me for thirty pieces of silver. My life might have some value to them in a land where God is picking sides in the great clash of civilizations. I ask the Soldier at the counter if I can take a taxi to a hostel and she says yes. She looks right through me and I climb into the first cab in the line.

The cab driver is a Sephardic Jew. He has dark skin and a hot wife. She's featured in the picture album he hands to me in the first few minutes of the taxi ride. I look at the pictures of their wedding celebration and wonder what happened to the bride of his childhood. Where is she on this January night? Is she looking at her parents' wedding album and wondering where he is? Did she even remember being married on that hot summer day? Did she marry for love or for the love of a wedding? I look at the pictures and grunt my approval at the appropriate places. I say she's a beautiful bride and the driver squints at the onrushing highway. He lives for this. From the pictures and the fact the driver is working the night shift, I can only imagine that she's gained forty pounds during their six-year honeymoon. But the driver still sees her in his highway mind as the thin woman with big breasts in a white dress.

I enjoy the foreign highway. Highways in the old world are identical to American interstates but with a few subtle differences. For instance, we pass an exit for Ancient Joppa. The word "ancient" has never been painted on an American highway exit sign.

I look up the word "hostel" in my Hebrew language guide. I arrive at the hostel with some apprehension. It's 9:00 p.m. and there's a line at the counter with four college students. I wait impatiently while they arrange for lockers and rooms. I pay my $20 and go up to the dormitory. There are six bunk beds in the room and all but one are full. I put my backpack on the remaining top bunk and head out into the Tel Aviv night.

It's warm for January. I walk past the restaurants that have thick black paper over their windows to deter young men with bomb vests from finding a Jew-rich establishment to target. I walk by the 24-hour sex shop that sells all kinds of sexual paraphernalia except for the most important sexual object—a live human woman. These are not for sale. It was B.Y.O.W.—Bring Your Own Woman—and I'm walking alone.

I walk into an empty bar and order a Goldstar. It's a decent beer, brewed in the Holy Land by the Hebrews, and I drink it in silence. I can read it's label, because the Hebrew letters spell out "Goldstar" in English. There are some benefits to four years of seminary education.

I ask the bartender if this bar gets crowded. With the Sabbath being the main weekly orientation in Israel, I can't figure out which day is the most likely club day. At midnight, the club is filled with young Jews. They're dancing and laughing with one another. The DJ plays some American songs and some Israeli dance hits. I move my feet to the music and feel old. The kids dance in their own circles and avoid me. I'm the tallest person in the small room. The most popular song is "*A Salaam Alekum*," which means "Peace be unto you" in Arabic. It's also the Muslim greeting. The Jewish kids go crazy when this song comes on. At least the youth of Israel are crazy about peace, I think. But then again, they're so young and most of them have never killed for their country. I leave and walk back to the hostel.

In the morning, I jog down a road by an ancient beach to work off my hangover from the night before. I think about all the twists and turns of my life thus far. It only takes a second to recount the major events that determined the facts and figures of my life. I can see all the years of my life from zero to thirty in the blink of an eye. Life is short, and I can't yet change the march of time.

The smells of the Middle Eastern city street remind me of Baghdad. I glance around and look for someone with a gun. A policeman opens his car door and stands behind the door as I jog down the street facing traffic. The cop brings the radio up to his mouth, and I dive into the street and roll behind a car. My knees are skinned on the gritty street, and I listen to my breathing. Somewhere in the middle part of my brain I heard, "Dive!" It's the voice that saved me in Baghdad. Now I can't stop it from trying to save me from the harmless world where I must live until my last day on the planet. I get up and run back to the hostel.

My backpack is still on the hostel bunk where I left it. Several of the college students are getting dressed for the day. They ask me where I'm from and I tell them I'm in the U.S. Army. Like most Americans from the Heartland, they are impressed. Most of them are students at a Christian college in Oklahoma. They're devout young men who are volunteering at the bomb shelters in the Jewish settlements near Gaza. They babysit children who live there while their parents work on the surface during the day. There's a war going on at this particular time. The Arabs are shooting rockets from their soccer fields into the Jewish soccer fields and homes.

I join them for a few beers in the lobby of the hostel. One of the students shares that he went to a Palestinian house in Gaza where the people had nothing to eat. There is a long, drunken pause. The guy restarts the story by saying that he went into a Palestinian's house in Gaza. Yes, yes, I say. He tells us about meeting a family who is hungry and poor, but they cook up and share some Russian rice and put salt on it for him. After each family member eats a small bowl of rice, he gives them his only candy bar. The mother breaks it up into seven pieces for each boy and girl in the family.

They all eat the half-melted chocolate and the son who was called little Mo (short for Mohamed) has chocolate running down the corner of his mouth. Our storyteller pauses and looks around the room. He continues his tale and says the mother reaches over and wipes the chocolate off his cheek with her finger. She puts the finger in her mouth and sucks on it. "Dude," he says, "she just did it." I think of my own kids. The horrible thought that they might be hungry strikes me as only the drunk can be struck. I tell the students they are brave and that they should be proud of what they are doing for these kids.

The next morning, I run with one of the students, but he soon tires of my relentless pace. He hasn't suffered enough to enjoy the monotonous pain of running. We read to know we are not alone. I run to learn to be alone. I walk back to the hostel with the guy as the temperature climbs into the high 90s.

The next day I meet with my father's tour group. He's in Israel to lead a group of parishioners on a tour of the Holy Land. I'm here to see him and participate in a portion of the tour. We travel on a bus into the Galilee and I feel good to be with these people who still attend the church I grew up in. For a few moments of the trip I feel like I'm home and safe, but maybe it's just because I'm so close to Baghdad.

We're all staying at a kibbutz on the Sea of Galilee. I'm told it's a freshwater lake that sits atop another layer of saltwater, way down deep. This fascinates me, the salt below the fresh. The pressure of the massive amount of fresh water pushing down on the saltwater, holding it in its place. There are things I can't know. All I know is that deep down, there is a salty darkness inside of me that is starting to mix with the fresh water on the surface. I've kept it down all my life and now the war has taken too much of the fresh and left me with too much of the bitter. I keep it down with my jokes, my smiles, and "I was only there for a year," but I can feel it coming up. I've touched the rage that lies beneath the thin veneer of what we call civilization. I know what is down below, so I turn from the lake and go to bed.

I get up early and I run in the dark along the edge of the Sea of Galilee. I stop at a site marked as the Baptism of Jesus by John the Baptist. I stop running and walk over to the stone building with a parking lot in front. Behind the building is the Jordan River and it's fenced. There's a fountain in front of the building with water from the Jordan. I bend down and put my head under the small channel of water under the fountain. It's still dark and the water is cold. I hold my head under the water. I stand up and the water from my head soaks my shirt. I am baptized. Somewhere further to the South, to the left of the main highway, the Jabbock Creek flows down out of the Jordanian mountains into the Jordan. I'm now a man of two baptisms. I've wrestled the man in the gritty shores of the creek, and now I've dipped my head in the clear, cold waters of the river.

My father and his tour group leave for Egypt in a few days and I'm alone in Jerusalem. I wander between the shrines of the three big Monotheisms. I circle the Old City three or five times a day. I wait to hear God speak. I wait for the unconditioned silence. But all I hear are buses, protests, and people just trying to make it in a town where religious organizations own over 70 percent of the land. I leave Jerusalem and get on a plane for D.C. I'm in the Holy Land only to realize there is no Holy Land after all.

Washington, D.C.: After Redeployment

The trip to Israel and Palestine has opened my eyes. Now, when I think of the Middle East conflict I can only think that there are beautiful women on both sides of the war. I meet my first Jewish girlfriend, Eva, at a bar downtown. She comes to the bar after attending a lecture on diplomacy and I'm there because I missed the departure bus for the mobile soup kitchen where I volunteer. I like to volunteer at the soup kitchen because I get to ride with another volunteer and that brings us together. I can also go out to a bar afterward and impress women with the soup kitchen stains on my sweatshirt. They are sexier than battle scars in this city.

After a few minutes of conversation at the bar, we head out into the night. I ask her if she is Jewish. She's from the former Soviet Union, and she's surprised that I can tell. I tell her I have good "Jew-dar." She likes this. I go with her on a Metro train that is headed for her stop in Virginia. I look her in the eyes and tell her I will turn 34 in seven days. She tells me that she's also 34. When I hear this, I close my eyes, lean over, and kiss her on the lips. I kiss her with an abruptness that surprises both of us. My eyes are still closed when the train stops suddenly at her station. She jumps off and heads to her apartment in Virginia, across the river.

I see her again a few days later. We have a good time, and I can't get over the fact that she is Jewish. I love it. I love her. The cold of winter sets in, and I'm at her place on Veterans' Day in November. Of all days, I know I deserve to have sex on this holiday. I have only had one real sexual encounter since my divorce, and that ended the relationship. We sit by the fire and stare at the tongues of the flames. They flicker and burn the wood to ash. I tell her I love her and we make love. I use a condom, and when it's over, I look down and see the condom lying there in the bed. It fell off.

I'm scared. I'm panicked. I say, "Jesus." She replies, "He's not going to help me. He's only going to help you, David." I lie down and stare at the ceiling wondering if my life has taken an irrevocable turn that I can't correct. I feel like the guy on the boat on the Niagara River. I feel like I've crossed the line where no matter how hard I paddle, I'm still going over the falls. I can't breathe. There's a tightness in my chest that doesn't go away with the dawn.

At work the next day I lead a spirituality group in the psych ward. I try to help the young men and women process the spiritual and religious changes that have taken place during their deployment and hospitalization. We are sharing Bible stories and placing ourselves in these timeless parables. On most days, I love this Ignatian spirituality. However, on this day, my mind is across the river in Virginia. I'm worried about whether I have a Jewish baby on the way.

My phone rings during the group session and I step outside the room to answer it. It's my Eva. I tell her she needs to buy the morning-after pill. She says it's already 2:00 p.m., almost a full twelve hours after our ill-fated lovemaking. I tell her it doesn't matter. I'll pay for it.

She calls me two hours later and tells me I don't have to worry anymore. She took the pill and everything's fine. I drive to her house after work and make love to her again. We hold each other after we finish, and she reaches over to the nightstand and lights a cigarette. She asks me if I smoke and I say, "I only smoke after sex." She laughs and says, "Sometimes I smoke instead of sex." She is the wittiest, smartest woman I've ever met. Everything that comes out of her mouth is profound. I'm in awe of her.

After we make love, she tells me she likes it from behind. I reveal to her I don't like that position so much. She looks at me quizzically and probes a little further by asking me if I associate the position with kneeling and all the spiritual and worship acts associated with it. I'm always amazed by her questions, the ways she quizzes the world. She always says she's an "Ah-theist," and I love how she says it in her barely detectable Russian accent. I assure her that's not it, I don't associate that with that, but I honestly don't know why. I feel exposed when I kneel in a bed, even with the curtains closed. I feel exposed all the time. I want to be good at all this but I'm a self-taught man with a fool for a teacher.

Eva has a PhD from Yale, and at 34 she wants to be married and have a baby. Her desires scare me to the core. I'm already married to my two sons and I can't add another. I can't do this for her. Our first sexual encounter was on November 11 and now it's December. Christmas is coming, and I write her a Hanukah song that weaves some Christmas themes into it. "Hold me when eight lights go out," I sing. There's a blizzard in the city a few days before Christmas Eve, so we trudge through the snow to go to church. She sings the Christmas carols at the top of her lungs. I take her back to her apartment, I pop a tiny pill, and we make love. All I want is someone to hold in the silent, cold night. I can see Joseph and Mary and their baby holed up in the stable. When the shepherds leave, it's three against the night. We hold each other, then I leave for Pennsylvania to see my boys. I call her later that week and tell her I can't give her a baby. I don't see a future for us. She agrees and says she doesn't want to spend New Year's Eve with me if I won't be with her in the New Year. From Joseph to David Peters, men have been scared of unexpected babies for as long as we can remember.

CHAPTER 8
Patricia

Washington, D.C.: After Redeployment

Most men think they know something about war, for they have seen movies. Most people can tell from a few details of my life that I've been in one or more. It's not hard to figure out. Sometimes I feel like a Vietnam vet in his O.D. Green jacket, sleeves cut off, patches everywhere, hoping someone will notice.

Men ask me what it was like to be in a war—what it was like to go through "that." I've lost all my good lines, all my good answers. I talk about the erosion of trust and how good it feels to know how you'll die. Then I'm quiet. All I can say is that being in a war for a year is like working in a brothel for a year.

War is like a brothel. A war has its own smells, its own touches. These are some things you can't learn about unless you're there. All the war movies in the world never smell like a war, they never feel like a war. I know what it smells like. I know how it feels. Nothing in this world smells or feels like that world. We fantasize about brothels like we fantasize about war, and we are wrong about both. When we know, we realize there are no more words.

Patricia is beautiful. In fact, she is the most beautiful woman I've ever met. On the day we meet I've been drinking out of a small bottle of Captain Morgan's rum in the town square of Columbia Heights, D.C. The splash pad fountains are gushing and my two boys are playing in them. I'm kicking a soccer ball to them and they're kicking it back to me. I'm wearing a Brasil jersey and having a good time. I see her. She's wearing a white blouse and jean shorts. She's encouraging her son, a boy of 4 years, to play soccer with me. I kick it to him. He kicks it back. I slowly roll it to him and he picks it up. He turns to his mother and smiles a mischievous grin. I look at her and smile. I turn and play in the fountain. I swing my boys around in the water and they're so happy to play with me. No one can create joy like a father at play.

I turn and her boy is there. He's kicking the soccer ball. I follow him and she's sitting on the edge of her seat. I look at her, at the boy, and then at the ball.

I say, "Hey, he likes soccer." She looks at me and says, "You like Brazil?" I say, over-pronouncing the "s", "Sometimes, but I really just like this shirt."

She laughs, even though I wasn't funny. I ask if this boy is her brother. She laughs, then blushes. She says, "No, this is my son Juan." "Hi Juan," I say. He's running back into the fountain with my soccer ball. My boys haven't noticed it's gone.

I turn to her and say, "I'm David, what's your name?" She says, "I'm Patricia." I look her in the eye and say, "Your son is a good *football* player." I return to the game where the rules are made by me. I play with my boys. I kick the ball to Joey. He laughs, then runs. I look at Patricia and smile. She smiles back. I sit down next to her while the kids play.

"Can I have your number?" I ask. She says, "Yes." Then she says, "He likes you." I feel strange. I look at my boys. I look at Juan and say, "He's a good guy." She says, "He's everything to me." I spin my boys around once more in the fountain's water, then we go home.

The next day I call her and ask if she wants to go to the movies or to the zoo. The National Zoo is about a half mile away. She says she wants to go to the Spy Museum. I say, "That's cool. We wanted to go, too." The next day we're all riding the bus to the Spy Museum, all five of us. She's cool and aloof. She's also beautiful. I look at her and look away. She speaks in clear, accented sentences. The boys have a good time at the museum. They're all fascinated by the spy gear or maybe our budding romance. They can see how I look at her. They know there's a shift in the universe. They know the seasons will never be the same again.

I go out with her alone. Her parents are watching her son and my boys are in Pennsylvania, 160 miles away from my apartment in D.C. I walk her down 14th Street to an Asian fusion restaurant where they have calamari. At the Spy Museum she told me she craves calamari. It's a beautiful restaurant. She sits with her back to the wall in a tight dress that flows into a looser skirt. It's brown, like her skin. She tells me what it's like to grow up in Puerto Rico. I say that it must be beautiful. She says, "After a while, it isn't beautiful. The beaches are so pretty they are sad." I look at her and say that she's beautiful. She looks at me and tells me she's been meeting with some Mormon missionaries. She says she won't have sex until she's married and she wants to wear nothing but jewelry on the night of her wedding, so all her husband can hear is the rhythmic jingling of her chains on the night that she first makes love. I'm captivated by this. She's the first woman who turns me on. Until now, I've been looking for safety in women, not beauty. The beautiful ones have always scared me. Patricia scares me now but I'm too drunk on love to feel the fear.

She's 27 and I'm 34 so I wonder about our long-term compatibility. I can find a flaw in everything. I call her and say to her mother who answers, *"Hola, este es David. ¿Puedo hablar con Patricia, por favor?"* She comes to the phone and tells me of her last boyfriend. He was Jamaican and yelled at her in front of The Diner in Adams Morgan, a neighborhood near me. We walk near there and she tells me the story again. On the phone she tells me she has some more things to tell me.

On Friday night I go to her house. She lives on the sixth floor of a D.C. apartment. Her mother and father live there, too. Her father is the maintenance supervisor for the whole building. It is a two-story apartment and we are touching each other in the kitchen. She tells me she is on probation. "Probation?" I say. "Yes," she says. "I hit my sister when she was holding her baby right here." She gestures to the end of the kitchen by the door. "She dropped her baby and the cops came." I just listen at this point. "I black out. That's what I do when I get angry." She told me how a falcon comes to her window every night and she tells him her dreams. She tells me she wants me to be her boyfriend. I live four blocks away and I like this idea. I can wait forever to have sex. I think I can wait until marriage if she is as hot as Patricia. That's what I think. Maybe I can be different too. She looks at me and says she is about to get off probation in a few weeks.

When she tells me she's on probation for hitting her sister, and by extension, her baby niece, a red flag erects in my mind and I think about having a wife or girlfriend who has been arrested for child abuse. My ex-wife might have something to say about this. Maybe I would, too. I don't know what to do so I listen. She tells me how she got fired from the Office Depot in the neighborhood. She says that she hit a black woman on the head with a stapler. *Yes*, I think. *I can see why you got fired for that.*

If she can't find work when she's off probation she'll go back to the gentlemen's club. She says she used to work there. She names the club. I know the place over on Connecticut in Adams Morgan. I've never been inside, but Patricia is telling me something, I know. She's saying I can save her. Her son's father is in a Puerto Rican prison. He gets out in about five years. I hope my sentence will be less than that, but I doubt it.

I go out with her again and she pulls me close and tells me that I'm her boyfriend. I feel a surge of pride in my chest. I look her in the eyes and she says, "Boyfriend, in my country, pays for everything. Girlfriend gives everything to him." I like that. I have money. I also have child support and two boys far away. I say, "That's cool," and I hug her.

My friend, Mike, has a pool at his apartment and we're all there. Mike, Patricia, her son, and me. We swim. We lounge. I crack open a beer and enjoy the afternoon sun and the beautiful pool. At that moment her son Juan runs around to the other side of the pool. I watch him as he runs. He jumps in. I know he can't swim so I jump in after him. When I pull him up to the surface he's gasping for breath. I look over at Patricia and she's talking to Mike. She's wearing a tight turquoise bikini. She's hot and I know it. I look at the pool again and Juan, her son, is jumping in the deep end again. I rescue him one more time. I strictly warn him against further self-destructive behavior. I walk them home and kiss her on the cheek goodnight. Juan's not the only one jumping in the deep end.

I call Patricia on the phone and she talks for 50 minutes. I reach my breaking point. I try to talk, but I can't. I spent a year on the phone with my ex-wife and it was all false. Where was she when I got home? Where was she when I felt like everything would fade to black? I talk to Patricia, but before long, I can't talk anymore.

When I call after a couple days she says, "Why you no call me?" I say, "I don't know." I say I want to come and see her. She lives four blocks away. It's about a seven-minute walk. She says, "No." Her parents are home. I drink some more whiskey. I go and drink with my friend, Mike, and his sometimes girlfriend, Messila, at Mike's apartment. She has a beautiful, goddess-like name, and I sometimes think of her and my friend, Mike, as my parents. I drink another shot of whiskey and head out when I see them start to touch each other.

I ride my bicycle to the next bar, the one a block from my house. It's

Friday night, but the bar is almost empty. I have a can of PBR for $1 and I'm so drunk I can't taste it. I say goodbye to the bartender and I bike home. All I remember is feeling like I'm falling.

I wake up and I'm sore. I sit up on my mattress. I look at my sheets and they're splotched with blood. I feel stiff and I have a splitting headache. I look around and I know it's Saturday morning. I see my bicycle in my apartment and I know I must have made it home. I look around and the pain in my side shoots through me like a blow from a baseball bat. I turn on my side and feel the pain shoot through me. I gasp. I look at my watch and realize two things. I realize I'm two hours late to pick up my kids. I also realize I can't remember the bike wreck. I vaguely remember the evening, the bike-ride, and the sudden stop when I hit the curb. I remember nothing after that. I feel ashamed and sad. I call my ex-wife to tell her about my lateness. She doesn't answer.

I tell my friend, Steven, what I did. He asked me why I was drinking. I said, "My girlfriend is saving herself for marriage!" "Oh," he said. That would explain everything. "There's your problem." I say to Steven, "Yes, I know." I know Steven. He lives a couple floors below me in my building. In his one-room apartment lives a woman who worked or works as a prostitute. He hired her, then took her in, so she could have a place to stay. Martini in hand, Steven often tells me on the stairs that "We are so close to a real breakthrough." Steven is exactly right. Patricia is offering me the classic Either–Or. If you give me marriage, I'll give you sex.

I go to Patricia's parent's apartment on Saturday night. Her dad is drinking and then disappears with his wife to their room. Patricia shows me some music videos of her on the Internet. A Columbian singer hired her to act in a music video. She's lying on pillows inside what appears to be a large martini glass. She is dressed in a bathing suit and high heels. There's another girl in the glass with her. My first impulse is to ask why there are pillows in the glass and not some kind of liquid. I think better of it and stay silent. As the song progresses, she begins to kiss the other girl in the glass. She stops the video and turns to me. "He said I would be famous." I look at her and say, "I think you are."

She asks me to help put her son to bed. I've already given him the "thumb jump" about a dozen times. I hold my thumbs out and he grabs them and he leaps into the air. Sometimes I spin him around. He loves all of it. He loves having a man around who will play these games with him. My boys are 160 miles away in Pennsylvania, sleeping like cherubs.

We put him on her bed and he falls asleep. Patricia walks towards her son's room down the hall. I follow. She goes in and sits on the floor. I do the same. She puts the movie *Cars* on the DVD player. The movie begins and Lightning McQueen begins to rev his engines. She looks at me. I'm sitting cross-legged on the carpeted floor, getting ready to watch a movie I've seen too many times. She reaches up and locks the door. She looks at me and puts her hands on my shoulders. I wrap my arms around her body. We kiss for the first time. I'm confused. I'm angry she told me she was saving herself for marriage. Initially I was relieved she said as much. Like everyone in a powerless situation, I made my peace with the idea. Now she's changing the deal and I'm disturbed.

Two nights before she asked me how many women I had sex with. I said about six or seven. I thought about it a little longer and said eight. She said she adds up her partners at the end of every year. When we met she had seventy-seven. No more, no less. I don't know what to think. Maybe that's why I drank so much the night of the crash.

Now she's pushing me down on my back. She pulls her skirt up and pulls off her panties. I kiss her with passion and fervor. I'm hard and I roll her over and my face hovers over. My body lightly touches her. I'm inside her and my mind is racing. I didn't bring a condom since we had an agreement to wait until we're married. She broke the rules, her rules, and I panic. I pull out and say I'm sorry. I leave her apartment. I walk past her sleeping father and her sleeping son. I walk past the picture she broke over her father's head. I walk past the place in the kitchen where she beat her sister with her fists. I walk the four blocks back to my apartment.

A few days later I call her. All she says is, "Why you no call me?" I see her and tell her I think we both need to move on. I say I'll be over in a few minutes. We sit in her living room and she tells me she is going on a religious retreat with her church, the Mormons. They will all live in cabins for a week. She says "cabeens" and I miss her. Her son takes pictures of both of us as we break up. This may be the only break-up of mine ever caught on film.

When I walk away I know one thing. Patricia is the first woman I dated on looks alone. She was so beautiful, in spite of her child abuse conviction, her probation, and her lack of desire to go to school. I'm proud I asked for her phone number.

CHAPTER 8
Caroline

Washington, D.C.: After Redeployment

I'm beginning to love my work at the hospital. The wounded warriors trickle in from the war and need just as much spiritual care as they need medical attention. I sit with them and they tell me about their women. They mourn the fact their wives and girlfriends don't want to touch them as much as they used to and that they can't get erections anymore. Everyone knows the last time they had one to the day. They confess the sins of war. They remember the children they shot and ran over with trucks. Running children over was common in a war where drivers are told to drive on, no matter who or what gets in your way. Every driver in Iraq must contemplate this choice—drive on or hit the brakes. They talk about the time they fell asleep while they were manning the .50 caliber and two men in their squad died. They confess the sins they committed before they lost their legs. Some of them know why they lost their legs and a few are sure it was a good thing. I never tell them that everything happens for a reason. They have the rest of the people in the world to tell them that.

But what if everything does happen for a reason? What if the universe works this way? What if God cuts the legs off a man who steals his mother's car and drives it from Phoenix to L.A. to buy drugs? What if God does this for a reason? What if He does this so the man won't steal any more cars from his mother? If God does work this way, what will I lose for my sins? What will God lose for his?

My worst fear was always torture. In Iraq, I worry I won't hold up under the pressure of pain if captured. The scariest movies and books are the ones where the dirty humans huddle together in a dirty pen, dreading the opening of the dungeon door. When it creaks open, they all shudder. Then the hand, or claw, or tongs reaches in to pick one out and carry her away to God knows what. The humans scurry away from the claw, but one is always taken and never returned. Beyond the dungeon is the trial by torture or sport killing. The humans run through a maze while a monster chases them in the dark. I know what scares me. God used to scare me. Sometimes He still does, especially when I feel His claw brushing my back, searching for His next experimental victim. I'm selected for some reason, unknown to me, and given to a monster of my own choosing, to play the gladiator in a battle I can't win. God watches from above for reasons known only to Him. The spotlight shines on me when the game nears its end.

I remember back to when I had been divorced for only a few weeks and I went to church with the woman I wouldn't call my girlfriend. It was a new, conservative Presbyterian church-plant in a hip neighborhood in Wilmington. No one owns cars here. It's time for the confession of sin, and I can't say it. I can't tell God that I have sinned against him in thought, word, and deed. I can't be sorry and truly repentant. I can only think, *I have nothing to confess. But you, Oh God, you have a few things to confess to me.*

At Walter Reed, in the amputee ward, every one of the wounded men has a story that connects them to the strong, indestructible warrior who won the reverse lottery of a roadside bomb. They show me pictures of their friends, their families, and their legs. They always want to show pictures of their legs. The pictures show them at the beach throwing a Frisbee. They're running. They're walking. They have legs and I get it. I know what they're trying to tell me. After this, I always ask how tall they are. I never ask how tall they *were*, but they always tell me their highest height, a minute before the bomb blew their leg to shreds of flesh.

The story that connects them to their indestructible self includes a moment when they thought they might die but refuse to let go. They hung on and survived. Like them, I will survive. I will be fierce and face the pain of the world. I will face my own pain. I will remember my death and survive. A man who survives war has two births—one when he is born and one when he faces death.

Baghdad, Iraq: Seven Months after Deployment

During my year in Iraq, I'm aided by a Soldier who is called the Chaplain Assistant. She's married to a sergeant who is spending his deployment in Kuwait. He comes up to Baghdad a few times, and I always encourage them to get together. They always do, I suppose, and I'm glad someone is getting it on in this Godforsaken place.

She goes with me to the gate where the Iraqi dump trucks bring gravel onto the base so we can keep our muddy roads passable. The Iraqi dump trucks are orange and all the drivers are dark and skinny. My Soldiers search the trucks and the drivers at the gate for bombs and who knows what else. My assistant and I walk over to a guard tower to visit with some of my Soldiers who spend the hot day watching the cars go by on the Baghdad street below. As we cross the gravel yard, a dump truck drives by and stops. The driver leans out the window and makes a hand gesture towards my assistant. He is pretending to jerk off a giant, imaginary penis. He's laughing. He laughs but he's too far away for us to hear. My assistant, Sandy, assesses the situation and raises her rifle and points the business end in his direction. He looks at the muzzle and slithers back into the cab of the orange truck. They never do this to her again.

On a hot day in Baghdad, we go and visit the gravel yard again. My Soldiers are there but it's quiet, and there aren't any trucks. I ask the Platoon Sergeant about the trucks and he takes me to the guard tower. He tells me what happened that morning. Parked in front of the gate is an orange dump truck. Sitting behind the steering wheel is a man. He is dead. He's been decapitated. His headless body is a warning to the other drivers. In a few days, the drivers return with their gravel and I look at them differently. I know they can picture themselves propped up, headless, behind their steering wheel.

Washington, D.C.: After Redeployment

The cherry blossoms are blooming and I begin my Saturday by walking to the Japanese store with a woman who slept over at my apartment. She's a friend of my roommate. We went out to a local El Salvadorian bar the night before, and we both got wasted. The last thing we do is dance to the Spanish karaoke music on an empty dance floor. Somehow, we make it back to my place, and make out for a few minutes. Then we sleep together fully clothed, observing the chastity of the drunk.

The Japanese store is a few blocks away from our apartment. The store is full of small plates and cups. I look around for a sake set and buy it. All I can hope is that some Japanese bowl or cup will attract a female if she sees it in my apartment. For some reason the white women I know are often attracted to Asian things but not so much to Asian guys. The woman I slept next to last night is running her hand through the kimonos on the other side of the store. I hold my credit card with both hands, bow, and present my card to the cashier. We walk out of the store and watch the traffic.

I go to work at the hospital and listen for an hour to a mother share about her son. She tells me in great detail how her son, a young man who lost a leg in Iraq a few weeks before, wants her to get married again. She tells me it's because he doesn't want her to die alone. After thirty minutes of sharing her dilemma, she pauses. She looks at me and says "We were born alone and we will die alone." I'm silent. She says, "That's what I told my son."

Her son, the young Soldier, has never been alone. He was with his battle buddies when he was blown up. He was with the medics and surgeons when they medically evacuated him from theater. His mother has been by his side from the moment he arrived at Walter Reed. In the Garden of Gethsemane Jesus is not afraid to die. He, like the Soldiers I love, is only afraid of being alone, forsaken. The Soldiers don't need the chaplain to tell them they'll survive this war or the next one. They don't need me to tell them that they'll be safe because God is with them. They're not afraid of death. They just need to be told that whatever happens, "I'll be with you and you'll never be alone."

In the afternoons, every couple of weeks, I give tours to groups and religious celebrities who come to Walter Reed to see the wounded warriors. Walter Reed sits next to Ft. Stevens, a Civil War battlefield. Its historic buildings have witnessed the suffering and joy of Soldiers since 1909. I show the groups the pictures of past presidents visiting the troops and crack jokes about how far the nurses' dormitories, built three wars ago, are from the Soldiers' barracks. I say I don't know about any secret tunnels.

We walk by the building with the cannonball from the Civil War embedded in the wall below the second-story window. I show them the green field howitzer that sits in front of the hospital by the flagpole. I tell them Walter Reed no longer fires the cannon every morning when the colors are raised, so as not to disturb the rest of the patients who have heard too many explosions in their short lives.

I remember the tours I gave in Baghdad. On Sundays I pack a dozen Soldiers from my unit in the back of a military truck (LMTV) and my assistant and I drive around the Baghdad Airport base where we live. We visit Uday's, or is it Qusay Hussein's house, where a Joint Direct Attack Munition, or "J-DAM missile" blew up his family when we shocked and awed them in the beginning. The missile didn't kill either of Saddam's sons. They weren't there that night, but I'm sure somebody was. The tan, stucco-over-cinderblock house is demolished. We go to the "Flintstone Village" by "Victory Over America" palace. The whole base is an abandoned wonderland of nonsense. Flintstone Village is what we call the strange creation that Saddam built as a summer home. It looks like a cheap mountain, full of caves, so we name it after cartoon characters from the Stone Age. Since the invasion, Soldiers and Marines have written their names in spray paint all over the walls. We climb all around this maze of cabins and sundecks overlooking the man-made lake. The water is a beautiful sight for the Soldiers on the tour. I explain what little I know about the history of Iraq and Saddam. By these stories I'm telling them that they are part of history.

The last stop before the Green Beans Coffee Shop near the headquarters is the bombed theater. Right around the time of the invasion a J-DAM missile hit the theater, killing everyone inside. I heard from the chaplain I replaced that it was a Baath Party meeting that got hit. Behind the bombed theater are the ruins of an indoor swimming pool. I take the Soldiers to the edge of the empty pool and show them some chipped concrete and a bloodstain. The bloodstain is about five feet from the bottom of the pool. I tell them the story that was told to me when I arrived in Baghdad. Somebody told the Americans, probably by cell phone, that the Baath Party leaders were meeting in this theater. It was, most likely, somebody who was here in the building. This is where they shot him after the bomb hit. I don't know if I believe the story, or any stories over here. I think the old rabbi was right, "God created man because he loves stories." Maybe our stories can save us from the meaninglessness of war. Maybe they can save us from the God who loves stories.

In Iraq, we write our stories on the walls. We spray-paint the walls of

Saddam's ruined palaces. We write emails to our families who strain their imaginations to picture us in a war. We write our stories on walls of the port-o-johns that dot the landscape of war. These poets of the port-o-john may be telling the story the best. "SGT Smith sucks cock." Then, inserted in a different hand, "Anyone's" between "Sucks" and "Cock." I move quickly in the port-o-johns, remembering always a Soldier from my battalion who was hit with mortar fragmentation while he was taking a shit in one. He said to me, "I wiped, pulled up my pants, then staggered out of the shithouse, and collapsed." We all want to die a hero on a white horse, or raising the flag over Iwo Jima, but not here, not with our pants down.

"Smelly E was here" shows up frequently in my area, just above the toilet paper dispenser. Names without meaning, phrases without meaning, hundreds of sick word combinations, drawings of penises, and doggerel cover the brown plastic walls of the shitter. Each word, each line, is read thousands of times by their captive audience. When we get home, some of us think about writing; some do, but we never get an audience like the shithouse poets over there.

Washington, D.C. After Redeployment

I don't like breaking up with women because it means someone else is now alone. I don't like to add to the numbers of lonely people in the world. I wish every woman I ever liked would write me a one-page essay after they dump me about why the relationship failed. I'd file them in a folder and learn a thing or two about relationships. After carefully reviewing the document and correcting any grammatical errors, I'd write the dissenting opinion and send it to her. I could point out some historical discrepancies and give some background information known only to me. Of course, I would have to write the one page for every woman I broke up with, too. I can only imagine what they would write in their rebuttal. The essays would only be linked by the anger of the wronged.

Breaking up is now an art for me. I can now identify the first traces of the fear that wells up in me when I'm entering the trap of a relationship. I pull back. There is a greater delay in text message responses. The calls get shorter. Then the day comes. I wait until we have a big event planned together. I talk about how excited I am to go. Then I drop the bomb. She goes about her day like the sailors at Pearl Harbor before the fighters attacked on December 7, 1941. I tell her, "I can't do this anymore." She cries, sneezes; one even threw up. The bodily reactions are always followed by the same question, "Are we still going to the event?" I try to look sad and say, "No, I'm not going, but you can go if you want. Here are the tickets." I don't know if this hurts me more than it hurts her.

This is the only way to protect my frail psyche. This is all I can do. I was hurt so bad that I'm now immune from feeling any hurt. I'm angry at women. How could my ex-wife have left me for that motherfucker? My anger doesn't make sense anymore and I'm afraid. I'm afraid of being angry forever.

I lock the door of my office and lie face down on the floor. I prostrate myself on the small carpet before God or before the idol of my own rage. Normally, this worship might be okay, but today I'm about five minutes away from a meeting with a married woman who works at the hospital. I hear the knock. I stand up and open the door. She has tears behind her eyes she's not yet given permission to flow down her face.

She sits in my office and talks about her boyfriend who is married to a woman who doesn't love him anymore. At first, when I counseled adulterers, I felt no sympathy for them. But after surviving my ex-wife's affair, something changed inside me. I listen to this woman describe how her husband stopped loving her. I hear the way she mimics the words he says to her, and how it sounds just like me. I can see my ex-wife sitting with her counselor and telling her side of the story. When I hear that voice, I know she has every right to leave him.

With all the adulterers I counsel, I'm always a bit surprised at how little remorse they feel. They all know it's wrong. Even after all the shit has hit the fan, they think the greatest wrongs have been done to them. They are adding and subtracting with a different system of mathematics altogether. On *The Jerry Springer Show* the husband rages, "Why did you cheat on me?" She always says, "You never listen to me!" This is the calculus of the adulterer. Society will never accept this calculus, but every adulterer knows its power.

Today, I've been called into my boss's office to explain where I am in my life regarding my divorce. Senior chaplains who have never been divorced see me as a novelty or a casualty. I reassure him that I'm fine. My boss listens and tells me his views on the subject. My boss asks me if I will take my ex-wife back if she was willing. I stare at him for a whole minute. I know it's a minute because I can hear the clock ticking behind me. It's an anniversary clock that symbolizes twenty-five, fifty, or a thousand years of marriage to the same woman. The clock is in a glass house, like all marriages are. The clock's hands move by the power of a battery that will run down long before the woman or the man will die. After sixty seconds I say, "I don't know," and leave the office.

I walk up the stairs to the hospital ward. I walk by the nurses' station and into a room where a young man sits. Rick lost his legs when an Explosive Formed Penetrator (EFP) blew through the steel skin of his bombproof vehicle in Afghanistan. The explosive material is packed inside a steel tube and molds into the shape of a cone. When the cone explodes, it forms a reverse cone and can penetrate any armor. The enemy started using the EFP the year I was in Iraq. I learned about them at the same time the Army learned about them. The strongest tank armor melts like butter when the molten copper plate from the EFP passes through the steel armor and into the flesh of men and women inside. I sit in a room with a man who lost his legs when the copper plate came to visit him.

When Rick lost his legs in Iraq, he had to apply his own tourniquet. Every solider carries one because the leading cause of death in this war is massive bleeding from an extremity. Before we're deployed, we're trained to put a tourniquet on our own arm and on the leg of a bleeding battle buddy. We're told to wrap the short belt around the man's leg or arm and twist the "windlass," the stick that tightens it, until the bright red bleeding stops. With a sharpie, we are to draw a large "T" on the casualty's forehead. Next to that should be the hour we placed the tourniquet. This is the way we save lives in combat. Walter Reed boasts a few quadruple amputees. Four tourniquets saved their lives.

Rick looks at me and says, "What's up?" I told him that I was just pressured to get back together with my ex after being divorced for a year. Rick laughs and says, "Now that's interesting." "Yes," I say, "It's interesting to me anyway." The young man, who is now four feet tall, stares at me with a look that I've only seen on the men who are missing both legs. A man with no legs has faced his own death and nothing surprises him. When a man looks down and doesn't see his shoes, but instead sees a twisted, mangled emptiness, it does something to his eyes forever. He looks at me with those eyes and says, "That's fucked up." I run my fingers through my Army haircut and think, *I'm just glad I had sex with her after she cheated on me.*

Rick tells me that he put his profile on eHarmony—an almost all-Christian site. His profile has been on the site for three months, but not one woman has contacted him. He says that chicks dig scars, but they dig legs even more. Rick believes the source of his datelessness lies in one cold, hard truth—he can't protect a woman and he would feel helpless in his wheelchair. "What woman would go out with a guy who can't fight some thug off?" he laments. "Yes," I say, "a warrior is only good at one thing." Rick is a warrior, but he lost his identity when the floor exploded. Is a warrior defined by his ability to kill, die, and provide? Is a man? When we can no longer do these things what does that life look like?

I stay in his room for another hour, and we talk about loss and how to escape it. Soldiers can postpone grief indefinitely with booze, drugs, and women. There's always the gun we can swallow and pull the trigger. We know how to solve problems with guns. Our families would get more than half a million dollars from life insurance and all would be well. But all would not be well. I know there would be that nagging thought in my mind right before I pull the trigger. I might even hear a voice tell me to stop, and I don't want to confront that voice, at least not yet. I know enough about suicide to know that I can feel its sweet seduction. I know that taste, the metallic taste of a pistol barrel, all too well. I know I will not leave my sons with a fierce goodbye. It would only prove to my ex that I'm crazy. She thinks I'm crazy. She proved that when she called the Walter Reed Chaplain's Office and complained that I might do something dramatic. It didn't help that it was on the day that an Army psychiatrist named Nadal Hasan at Fort Hood shot more than a dozen Soldiers.

I know I have problems. I know I weep uncontrollably sometimes. I have a restlessness inside me that all the running and sit-ups in the world can't quell. I'm a caged animal in an invisible cage. Every morning in the Psych Ward at Walter Reed the Charge Nurse goes around the room and asks everyone to state their name and their mood. Staff members, the sane ones, are supposed to state their name and their occupational specialty. The patients say, "Hi, I'm Jon and I'm feeling...mixed emotions today." It helps that they have a laminated paper with a list of emotions on it. Above each word is a little round face that seeks to artistically capture the feeling. Some are better than others. Each staff member says, "Hi, I'm Dr. Smith, and I'm your attending physician." I say, "Hi, I'm David, your chaplain, and I'm feeling anxiety and hope today." Most days I feel like there's a thin line between the patients and me. I know that the feelings that I feel, if voiced, could land me in this place. I would stay for a few weeks and be medically retired from the Army. I wouldn't have to worry about financial matters anymore. I could just be "troubled" and "dark." I turn my head away from this bittersweet cup every time it presents itself. I want to be whole. I want to be okay. I want to be normal, even though I know I never will.

I'm jealous. I want to be a patient. I want to push the call button and summon a nurse to my bedside. I want the President of the United States to visit me and shake my hand. I want Fleetwood Mac and the L. A. Lakers to enter my room sheepishly and say "Thanks for all you've done for us." I avoid the celebrities as they visit the wounded warriors on Ward 57. They come every day to see the wounded. In 2009 I ran the Boston Marathon in 2:54, but today I'd trade that for a missing leg and some sympathy.

Baghdad, Iraq: Months after Deployment

All the great war stories have blood in them. This is what makes them worth listening to. I grew up in the USA where we buy our chicken breasts boneless, bloodless, and wrapped in cellophane. War is the only place where people who grew up in such a land can see blood pulse out of a jugular vein or a femoral artery.

There's a story full of blood I can never tell for it makes me look bad. I was walking through the Tactical Operations Center (TOC) when everyone looks up at me as if I'm expected. A sergeant comes to me and in a hushed tone that is reserved for news about death, he asks me if I heard. "Heard what?" I ask. The sergeant tells me there's been a suicide in Echo Company. "Who was it?" I say. They look at the floor and say, "It's Carmen Santos." The first name throws me and I can't re-pronounce it. "Carmen?" I said. "Yes," said the young Soldier who is staring at me like I'm a fucking idiot. "That's his name." I know Carmen, but I know him as Specialist Santos. I don't know his first name and he doesn't know mine, or anyone else's tonight.

I knew this young Soldier for about two years. He was at FOB Falcon on the other side of Baghdad when he did it. And so my worst war story begins for me. I plan the memorial service to be held at the chapel on the FOB. The Division Chaplain tells me the Division Commander issued an order that no honors would be rendered to Specialist Santos because he committed suicide. I suppose the general believes his Soldiers will be less likely to kill themselves if they know they won't get a 21-gun salute.

The chapel is packed with members of Specialist Santos' company. They all sit with their weapons on the floor between their feet. I give the memorial message. From the platform, I look out at the silent warriors who never sit in church unless blood has been spilled. I ask them if they know why Carmen has given us this fierce goodbye. I read the words of Jesus who says that God knows when the sparrows fall. I ask, "What sound does a sparrow make when he hits the ground on his last flight? A sparrow only weighs five or six ounces. Does God hear the sound of a five-ounce bird hitting the ground? Did God hear the sound of this man's fall?"

We are so full of questions. Why didn't he tell us he was hurting? I know Carmen was alone. In my mind, I see him walking to the Internet Café. What he read there I'll never know. Did his fiancé break up with him in an email? Did he chat with her and then she signed off too early? Did he see a picture of her with another guy on the Internet? He walks back to the empty barracks and lies down on his cot. He puts one round in his M16 and opens his mouth. The barrel of the rifle goes in. He closes his mouth around the steel that has been warmed by the Iraqi sun. He pulls the trigger but doesn't hear the sound. Does God hear the sound?

When his Platoon Sergeant and Squad Leader come back to the barracks, they think he's sleeping. They plan the next day's mission and discuss some equipment that's been damaged. It's only then they realize Specialist Santos is dead. Was it the angle of his feet on the cot that gives them the sense they were in the presence of death? All the dead we see in the movies are really live actors pretending, but every human knows what death looks like when they see it in real life. There's something about the twist of the neck or the way the knees are slightly bent that tells us deep in our soul that this human is no longer one of us. We know they have crossed the line, and left the small minority of humans that still breathe and breed. The two sergeants know this, and then they see the blood still dripping on the floor from his wasted skull.

This is the second time Specialist Santos had been deployed to Iraq. After months of combat and risking his life on the roads of Baghdad, he dies. There is no bugler playing taps at his memorial ceremony. The twenty-one guns are silent at his memorial, but everyone hears the single shot he fired as he lay on his cot in the last seconds of his life. When I visit his grave in Detroit, the caretaker at the cemetery tells me his father visits every day. Not all the casualties of war are made so by the enemy.

Washington, D.C.: After Redeployment

My girlfriend, Caroline, understands death. She gave birth to a daughter and a son, and she has felt another die inside her. She is drawn to death as she is drawn to life, my life. In her post-Christian, Buddhist heart, she knows that all happiness is mixed with sorrow. Caroline and I share a love of depth psychology. It's that subject we discuss in the hallway by my office on our first meeting. Like Freud and Jung, we go on and on for hours with tangents that defy sense and sensibility. She's pursuing me and I know it. I let her chase me because I trust her with my heart. I need someone to rescue me from the cold of January and the Russian steppes of my loneliness. She understands warriors. She knows we sometimes need a woman to take the pain away.

A few weeks later when we are watching a movie at her house, through invisible and unseen signals, I ask her put her head on my shoulder. She feels safe and I like her long hair lying across my chest. She is short, beautiful, and has blue eyes. She hates war but wants to be involved. She's drawn to war like a moth to the flame. I embrace her and her contradictions as she embraces mine.

I begin to love her because she understands the burden of being a single parent. She had both her babies when she was a teenager. She's been a single mother for seventeen years and her children are about to leave the house. She's my age and almost an empty nester. Her son is a grown man in my eyes. He's the age of my Soldiers. I feel sheepish when I'm having sex with his mother while he sleeps in the next room. After a few nights with her I can't sleep in her apartment when he's there. I think this is why I'm having trouble with sex again. Then I realize I'm terrified of having a baby with her or any woman. I remember the morning after pill and staring at the ceiling in the dark. I don't trust condoms so I schedule a vasectomy.

The physician's assistant who interviews me makes it clear that the vasectomy is irreversible and I will never have any more children. I nod with a knowing look and ask him how soon I can get the surgery. I'm a single chaplain and everyone knows this. I just smile back at them.

On the day of my surgery, I show up early and put my feet in the stirrups in the operating room. The nurse gingerly washes my balls. She throws them around so as not to arouse me. It works. This is the only part of the surgery that hurts. The surgeon comes in and sits down. I can see his head between my knees. After the shot of anesthetic in my ball sack, I feel nothing. When he says it's all over, I carefully get up and pack my package in frozen peas. My friend, Steven, drives me back to my apartment. Caroline takes care of me while I recover. She encourages me to take the pills that make me sleep. I don't remember anything about those next two days. I know she's cooking something elaborate she loves, but I have no memory of seeing or eating it. I drift in and out, but mostly out.

She's happy I'm getting the surgery because it means that she and I will never have a baby or an abortion. I'm not sure which she or I is more afraid of having.

Two weeks after the vasectomy, I must prove to the doctor that I'm no longer able to sire a child I show up at the clinic to make a semen donation for the cause. A nurse takes me to a back to an unmarked room and shows me how to work the VCR. He also points out a stack of magazines under the VCR. I'm amazed that this "jerk-off" room exists in the hospital. Unfortunately, the porn doesn't work for me. After watching a giant penis penetrate a vagina for about a minute I'm turned off.

I pick up a magazine instead. The date on the cover is 1975—the year I was born. I think of my parents making love the year this magazine was published and I lose my erection. I turn the lights off and use my fertile imagination. I channel surf in my mind until I land on the right memory.

A few minutes later, the sample is complete. I leave the room and carry the specimen to the elevator that will take me to the laboratory in the basement of the building. I turn my sample in to a young Soldier who is a professional laboratory technician. I can't help imagining him getting a good laugh about the chaplain's seed. A day later, I'm cleared to have unprotected sex by a board-certified physician.

Sometimes Caroline sleeps at my studio apartment I share with my 23-year-old roommate. He and I both sleep on foam mats on either side of the one big room. His girlfriend lives there too, and we share the small space with cheer. When I tell people that I share a studio with a 23-year-old roommate and his girlfriend, everyone always asks me if we are in the same room when they have sex. I always say, "It's all good. Don't worry about it." Sex is nothing to worry about.

Baghdad, Iraq: Months after Deployment

My war is full of contradictions. I think of the laser beams we use. About halfway into my tour, they give us laser pointers. The Soldiers in the turrets use them to ward off approaching vehicles when we are on a convoy. They shine them into the cars that come too close and the cars veer away. The Iraqi drivers believe they are lasers from weapon scopes or something. I think, but I'm not sure, that they can see they are just handheld laser pointers. This is, after all, a country where many homes have cable TV and indoor plumbing. They have cell phones but unreliable electrical service. These are the contradictions of a nation too long at war with her neighbors and the world.

My Soldiers shine their laser beams into the cars and no one dies. Shortly after I'm on a convoy, I notice that all the Humvees have sirens and police lights on them. The order came down from division to equip each vehicle with police equipment. I look for the box of donuts in the cab of the vehicle. Now, when we roll down the roads of Baghdad, the noise of our sirens precedes us. Cars pull over to the side of the road while their drivers give us dirty looks.

I only drive one mission in Baghdad. To my knowledge only a few chaplains drive Humvees during 2006 in Iraq. Chaplains are different from the rest of the Soldiers. Since we are noncombatants, we don't carry weapons. Even though the Geneva Convention states that we can, we have chosen not to. During the Vietnam War, some magazine put a picture of a chaplain on the front cover draped in machine gun bullets. Since then, we stay away from carrying weapons.

I drive a Humvee with a .50 caliber machine gun on the roof. We have intercom headsets and my Chaplain Assistant, Sandy, is my TC (Tank Commander). Non-tankers like us borrow the cool names. We are the third vehicle in the convoy. We are a gun truck that is supposed to protect the Logistics Convoy (Log Pack) that is carrying supplies to a distant FOB. We drive south on Route Tampa. On one side of the road, there's a wasted and burned tractor trailer that has flipped on its side. It was blown up by an IED the night before. Its cargo of bottled water is blasted across the shoulder and embankment of the highway. Bottles are everywhere. The cab is charred. It doesn't look like the driver survived. He was more than likely Indian, Pakistani, or another of the third-country nationals who do the real dangerous work here. Most of them make the minimum wage for their country and many of their recruiters keep most of their income for themselves. We rarely interact with them on the FOB unless they are doing our laundry.

Our convoy survives the trip to the distant FOB and we turn around and go home. We slow down and roll through an Iraqi checkpoint. I'm driving and my assistant is in the passenger seat. She is looking for IEDs. At the checkpoint, there's an Iraqi man in his late sixties standing there arguing with the Iraqi soldiers. He's waving his hands wildly, which may not necessarily mean he is angry. As we approach this exchange, the young Soldier who is arguing with him looks at me. Then he looks at my female assistant. He gets a look on his face that can only mean he wants to impress this American woman. He makes a fist and punches the old man in the stomach. The old man is wearing a long white robe and the young Soldier's fist causes the robe to billow. Then the fist connects with the old man's stomach. The old man doubles over in pain and we leave the checkpoint. In this moment, as I witness the least serious attack of the war, God dies. The God of my childhood, with His right and His wrong, drifts away like the air that billowed out of the old man's robe. All that's left is the dust and the heat and the war. As the God of my childhood floats off, another takes His place.

This new God can't care if people have sex or if they kill each other. The God of love and war only cares about humans being themselves. His glory is the human person fully alive and He knows that war is the only place where warriors feel fully alive. The God of love and war doesn't believe in good and evil but allows civilians to believe in such things. Warriors and lovers never believe in either. All is fair in love and war and, although this is often quoted, it's rarely believed by those who are afraid to inflict pain on another person. All the lovers who have left husbands and wives are convinced it was the right thing to do. The consequences, be they harsh words or the Scarlet Letter, are worth it.

All the warriors know that when a 19-year-old man has to shoot a nine-year-old girl because she's being used as a human shield, that there is no real morality in the world. The warrior knows the right thing is always right but it will haunt him forever. One second after the Soldier's thumbs depress the triggers on the side of the .50 caliber machine gun, the girl is cut in half. The bullets are six inches long. One second after the girl dies, the Soldier knows there's no right or wrong, only war. He'll see this girl in his nightmares for the rest of his life. Her life is now connected to his.

One such Soldier tells me about her on a summer afternoon at Walter Reed. I listen to his story. I spend the next day trying to help him embrace this girl. He's running from her, but she keeps following. He wants to take a shotgun from his gun cabinet, put the barrel in his mouth, and pull the trigger. He knows how easy it was to pull the trigger and kill the girl. He's tried it once before.

I try to help him look at the girl and not run from her. He can see himself turning towards the little girl who is following him. When she's close, he hugs her. They are one now and always will be.

Fort Hood, Texas: Months before Deployment

They come and get me one morning at 4:15 a.m. when I'm still at Fort Hood, Texas before I deploy to Iraq. I report to the Casualty Notification Office and get the file of the family I will tell about a death in Iraq. I'm notifying an ex-wife and her son that an ex-husband and father died in combat.

I get in the van with the Sergeant First Class (SFC) who is the Notification Officer. It's his task to be the first to ask the question at the door. He will ask if he is speaking with Jane Smith and if he can come inside. When two men show up at an apartment at 6:00 a.m. on a Saturday with their shiny brass buttons and green suits, it can mean only one thing—that death has come to call. All the wives and parents are told that the death notifications only happen between 6:00 a.m. and 10:00 p.m. at night. My wife told me that while I was deployed, she would look at the clock at 10:00 p.m. and breathe a sigh of relief. Every other knock on the door before 10:00 p.m. could be the angel in green with those shiny buttons.

I stand at the door of the apartment. We knock. The sergeant rehearses his lines. "The Secretary of the Army has asked me to express his deepest regrets that your husband, Staff Sergeant John Smith, was killed in action on 19 August 2005 in Baghdad, Iraq." After knocking for twenty minutes, we leave and get a coffee at McDonald's, to wait for their return. The sergeant keeps saying his lines out loud. He's scared. We bide our time. We won't give our position away. We will, like Death himself, show up when the family least expects it.

In a military community our task can't be any less private. We sit in the McDonald's and drink coffee to stay awake. We weren't sleeping well with the duty phone before it rang. Then we were up before the sun and fatigue is setting in. We sit in our uniforms and everyone looks at us with pity and understanding. The kind eyes take some of the edge off the morning and then it becomes too much. We leave and sit in the government van in front of the apartment building. It's always a van and it's always an apartment building.

At 9:00 a.m. we go back to the house and knock on the door. This time a woman comes to the door and she screams, "Oh, my God!" when she sees us. She knows and the sergeant feels guilty. I can see this by looking at the sergeant's face. It's a look of disgust and panic. He's faced many things, including the enemy, but now he's the enemy. He's face to face with a woman who has just lost something in war. She turns abruptly and we follow her in. She sits at the small glass-topped kitchen table and the sergeant and I sit across from her.

When we sit down, the sergeant mumbles his lines and the woman listens.

When the sergeant is finished, we look at her. Her eyes are fixed on the basket of small gourds that is the centerpiece of the table. All three of us stare at the gourds. Then she picks one up and throws it across the table at us. It misses us and hits the living room wall a few inches from the large plasma screened TV. Then she weeps. She weeps in angry sobs. She says that she doesn't want to tell her son. Then she stops and looks up and says, "My son, our son, is developmentally disabled and, even though he's seven, he might not understand."

The sergeant is eyeing the door. I ask her if there is someone I can call to come over to the house. She says she'll take care of that. I hug her and say nothing because there is nothing to say. I think she might feel the buttons on my jacket. Maybe it will remind her of an embrace in better times with her Soldier who captured her heart but couldn't keep it.

Something happened between then and now. It was only for a time. Something changed between them. Now, all that exists is a child that might not understand his own father's death. There's also more than $400,000 of Serviceman's Group Life Insurance that she will keep in trust for her son's 18th or 21st birthday, depending on the box the Soldier checked only days before he went to Iraq.

The sergeant and I drive back to the Casualty Notification Office. I thank the sergeant for doing such a good job with this notification. The chaplain isn't there to comfort the bereaved. The chaplain is there to comfort the one who makes the notification. The sergeant shakes his head and sighs. We both stare at the road knowing we're on call for six more days. This could happen again and again. We both wonder what kind of men we will be when it's over.

I do more of these visits in the years following this visit, but I never remember any of them. I only remember this one notification because of the gourd she threw when words were not enough. I will always know it was in autumn.

Washington, D.C.: After Redeployment

At Walter Reed I sit with a young Marine who is now an amputee. He tells me about his Alive Day—the day he died a few times and came back. He begins to tell me the story of how four Afghan soldiers carried him to the chopper after the attack. One of them got tired, let go of his stretcher handle, and he rolled off the stretcher and hit the ground with his mashed stump. He was wide awake and in pain for the hour-long flight to the hospital. Next to him on a stretcher was his Platoon Sergeant who died in the same attack. The Marine says he looked over and saw him breathe his last. "He never called for his mother," he says. "Maybe they didn't get along."

The Marine tells me he deals with the pain of his amputation by counting. He counts to a thousand sometimes. But the counting Marine tells me he is happy. He's happy he has a reason to live now that he lost his leg. People are offering him jobs, his fiancée is great, and she even loves his daughter.

Before his deployment he worried constantly about money. Now he has a guaranteed income for life. Maybe when we hit the bottom, the ground is finally solid enough for us to stand, even if it's on one leg.

The most obvious wound in the world is an amputation. Everyone sees it and knows how it happened. The hospital is full of young men with missing legs and arms in various stages of recovery. Of course, none of them ever recover the leg or the arm. All they get is a $50,000 fake leg that has to be painstakingly attached if the man wants to leave the house. Their titanium legs carry them and they carry their legs.

Celebrities come to visit them and sign pictures. The amputees are treated like celebrities. Their missing leg is their ticket to respect. While the amputation is the most visible wound, I can see a deeper wound. It's the wound that led them to Iraq or Afghanistan in the first place. It's the wound that numbered them among the phony tough and the crazy brave. It's the wound they refuse to clean. It becomes red and inflamed. Then the girlfriend, wife, or mother storms out of the room and won't talk to them for days. They weep for their wounds because they will never be healed. Someone at a party says, "When were you in Iraq?" All I can think is, *I've been in Iraq all my life.*

Ocean City, Maryland: Summer 1989

I remember my father preaching a sermon in the fundamentalist church of my youth. My dad says that time doesn't heal all wounds. Only the clean wounds heal. Yes, my father knows about wounds. Like the God he worships, he lost a son on this planet. His fourth son fell while he was riding his bike. As he was falling, a city bus ran over his head. There wasn't a sound. Just the airbrakes blowing and hissing as the driver slammed on the brakes. Witnesses say the bus driver just gripped the steering wheel and repeated, "Did I hit him? Did I hit him?"

My family grieves around me as I enter my teen years. They cope with their loss by saying it was God's will that he was taken to heaven. I can only think that God allowed him to die. In my 13-year-old mind I see God blowing a gust of wind to push my brother's bike over. The bike blows over and the head of the 7-year-old hits the asphalt at the precise moment the bus tire rolls over his head. I wonder if God called him, nay, commanded him, to wobble his handlebars and take the fall on the street. The God of the road is the God of war and He likes children, especially the dead ones.

I carry a dead body on my back, visible to everyone but me. Every time I drive a car, I think of that day in the fall of my freshmen year of college. I'm driving to church, a little under the speed limit. As I enter a sharp curve in the two-lane road, my driver's side front tire catches the median's curb. I overcorrect my steering, and see a red jeep on my right. I swerve back to the left lane and the front of my car crashes into a six-inch-high steel plate on the median curb. The front of the car is smashed and the wheels will not turn. Centrifugal force propels me into the oncoming lane of traffic.

The car is still moving. I look through the windshield of my 1973 Volkswagen Bug and see the lone headlight of a motorcycle. It's coming straight towards me. I turn the wheel, but the front of the car is crushed. The dashboard has compacted into my knee and fractured my kneecap, but I don't feel it. I don't remember anything after I see the headlight of the motorcycle. I wake up with shattered glass in my mouth. My hands are covered in blood.

When I get out of the car, the highway is silent. Traffic has stopped. I limp over to where I see a person lying on the ground. Even though she's wearing a motorcycle helmet, I know she's dead. I don't know how I know this. I turn around and see the motorcycle driver lying on the ground. A pool of blood is spreading from beneath his stomach. I instantly think this is where the handlebars hit him. He looks up at me as I come up to him and he says, "Fuck you, man." I say, "Yes." I can't think of anything else to say. In an instant, the paramedics arrive and we're all taken away.

For days I see that headlight coming toward me. I refuse to drive a car for four months. I still hate driving cars. The dead girl was the motorcycle rider's girlfriend. Maybe he still hates me for what I did. Maybe this is why I'm good at what I do. Maybe I can sit in the presence of death because death is always with me.

Washington, D.C.: After Redeployment

I now know I want to disappear for a while. That's the real purpose of the Death Letter. I want my sons to know why I disappeared if I come back too late or not at all. I don't know where I'll go, but I know the time has come. I want to leave the country and go somewhere where no one speaks English and no one calls me Chaplain.

I look in the mirror and see my face for the first time in weeks. I notice my hands are leaning on the sides of the sink. The face in the mirror is crystal clear but it isn't mine. It's the face of God.

Everything I do now is preparation for that day when the books will be opened and God, Bob Dylan, or my ex-wife will read off my sins. The truth will be told. All I can hope for on that day is that a woman will step forward in my defense. Maybe there will be more than one? Maybe there will be twenty or thirty of them there to tell the Universe who I am. Maybe they will share the moments of grace that each one experienced with me. This is all I can hope for when he comes again to judge the living and the dead.

I think I'm ready to tape this one to the back wall of my locker.

EPILOGUE

"People are not snapshots, they are moving pictures," said my professor, Thomas George, JD, PhD, one night in class. *Death Letter: God, Sex, and War* is a snapshot of my life in the days after my experience in Iraq. Today, I am thankful to say that I'm no longer there. The world I inhabited during those days was full of roadside bombs, Jager bombs, and F-bombs, none of which are socially acceptable outside the military community. I was afraid to publish *Death Letter* because I'm a spiritual and religious leader. As a leader I am often expected to be an example of pristine perfection. Instead of perfection, I want to be an example of hope. There is hope for all of us who have lost something in war.

With the encouragement of my wife, Sarah, and a number of combat veterans, I decided to publish the manuscript I tried hard to forget as I moved on with my life. I took a step of faith to publish this book, in hopes it would reach the people who needed to read it.

I will always remember what a dear chaplain friend and mentor said in an Easter Vigil sermon in Baghdad, Iraq, in 2006. "We live in a Good Friday world, but we are an Easter People." Truly, *Death Letter* is a description of my Good Friday world. "Easter" for me, came from a renewed relationship with the Church of Jesus Christ. I wrote most of this memoir as a journal in the months after I returned home. Since then I've experienced reconciliation, healing, and hope. The first place I found healing was The Episcopal Church. The bishops, priests, deacons, and laypeople believed in my call to the priesthood and challenged me to grow and heal so I could minister in the vineyard. While in D.C., I went on pilgrimages to the National Cathedral in D.C., I prayed the Daily Office and made my confession devoutly kneeling. I found acceptance and welcome in a community that recognized at once the profound harmony and disharmony of the world. Healing, for me, is restoration to the community I lost in war. I found that community in The Episcopal Church. Years after the events of *Death Letter*,

I was ordained a priest in Washington, D.C., just a few miles from Walter Reed Army Medical Center.

During my journey back to the Church, I found healing in my relationships with God. My relationship with God was severely strained by my experience in war. It took me a long time to come back to a place of faith and trust in God, Father, Son, and Holy Spirit. This healing happened slowly, and it's still happening in my soul as I journey into a deeper relationship with God through Scripture, worship, prayer, and contemplation. I know God spoke to me on the night I told him how I felt. I know Jesus suffered on this planet, which made my suffering have meaning. On the night he was betrayed he took bread, and every time I receive communion, I take a step toward healing. I know the Spirit moves within me and my community, taking us places we are afraid to go, even to the place where I published *Death Letter*.

Another place I found healing was with my ex-wife. After reading *Death Letter* the reader may jump to the conclusion that my ex-wife is the villain of the story. If there is a villain in my story it isn't her. It's the devil, or Mars, the god of war, not my ex-wife. I see her several times a week as we parent our boys and I enjoy discussing their growth and development with her. I'm thankful that she cares for our children. We aren't friends on Facebook or in real life, but she does her best to keep the peace with me and do what is best for the boys. A friend of mine says that in every divorce there's his side, her side, and the truth. What I wrote in *Death Letter* were *my* feelings about her. I healed from the betrayal of the affair slowly, and I'm still on that journey. I haven't started *Life Letter* yet. Maybe someday I will.

Most of all, my wife, Sarah, has given me a new vision for the healing gift of love. We married in the presence of God and our community and I treasure the vows we spoke that day and the hearty response of our witnesses who said, "We will!" when the question was asked them, "Will all of you do all in your power to uphold these persons in their vows?" I look forward to living the rest of my life in her love and presence.

I'm proud of my parents for loving me, even though they didn't always understand me. They gave me shelter when I needed it most and prayed for me every day of this journey. My parents have been fantastic grandparents to my children, and I was overjoyed to see them come and celebrate my marriage to Sarah.

I found healing when I learned how to write. The Veterans Writing Project and the Walter Reed Writers Workshop gave me an opportunity to write about my experiences. These two groups showed me the healing power of writing. At each meeting we would all bring in a few paragraphs and read them aloud. Those were holy moments of healing for me.

This project has been blessed with two expert editors, Leah Lakins and Sarah Bowen. Their painstaking attention to detail and their insistence on clarity helped me become a better writer. Any mistakes in *Death Letter* are entirely my own.

Like so many of my ideas, the first part of the title, *Death Letter*, popped into my head while I was running one morning. The second part of the title is inspired by Elizabeth DeOreo, a friend and psychiatrist at Walter Reed. Upon my departure from Walter Reed, she gave me a copy of John Irving's *A Prayer for Owen Meany*. On the inside cover she wrote, "For David, a delicious mix of God, Sex, and War."

Erik Shaw, CEO and founder of Tactical 16 Press, believed in *Death Letter* and made the project happen. Erik's wise counsel and patience gave me the strength to tell my war story. I'm also thankful for Bryan Dolch's thoughtful work on the cover design, and all the help I have received from the whole team at Tactical 16. Extra-special thanks for this reprinting of *Death Letter* goes to Army veteran Ben Keen and his organization, Steel City Vets. Groups like Steel City Vets are doing amazing work reconnecting OIF/OEF veterans with the communities that sent them to war. Every person who made this book possible serves veteran writers, their readers, and the United States of America.

So many other people have helped me on my journey home from war. I'm thankful for all of you. Most of you never knew you were helping a troubled veteran heal from his experience with war.

I'm also grateful for the many writers who read my work and encouraged me to keep working. Robert Johnson taught me how to write in the veterans writing course at Walter Reed and Ron Capps opened me up to a world of writers and readers. The most notable of these is Jeffrey Bartholet. Jeff is a writer who, at the time, was the Washington bureau chief for *Newsweek*. His coaching and encouragement helped me to, in Jeff's words, "Always write the truth," which is exactly what I have done in *Death Letter*.

APPENDIX
Paul Tillich and I Come Home From War

I never met Paul Tillich, but I feel like I know him. I met him, or at least the part of him that exists in books, when I came home from Iraq. All I knew of Paul Tillich before Iraq was what I heard in seminary about him. My professor of historical theology said of Tillich, "The man had a huge collection of pornography." Once I heard that, I wrote him off forever, or at least until I started living his life.

Like me, Tillich served as an army chaplain in a losing war. His war was World War I. In 1916, as Tillich marched with the German army toward Paris, German Chief of Staff Erich Von Falkenhayn, wrote to the Kaiser and urged him to approve his plan to attack Verdun, France. He promised this action would "Bleed the French white."[1] Thus the brutal battle of attrition began that resulted in the deaths of hundreds of thousands of men, a whole generation wasted in the bloody mud of France. On the German side of the battle of Verdun, in the rat infested trenches on the edge of no-man's land, Tillich served. He nurtured the living, cared for the many wounded, and buried the dead with his own hands in shallow graves.

Tillich was 29 when Germany invaded France in August 1914. I was thirty the day I set foot in Baghdad. In October of 1914 Tillich left his job as Assistant Pastor to join the army that was promised to "be home before the leaves fell."[2] World War I became "the turning point in Paul Tillich's life—the first, last, and only one."[3] I don't have a biographer yet, but I'm pretty sure Iraq was my first, last, and only one, too.

I left my job as Minister of Youth at a church in Pennsylvania to join the

---

[1] Don Arther, "Paul Tillich as a Military Chaplain," paper presented at the annual meeting of the North American Paul Tillich Society, Boston, (November 1999), 2.

[2] Arther, "Paul Tillich as a Military Chaplain," 3.

[3] Wilhelm and Marion Pauck, *Paul Tillich: His Life and Thought* (San Francisco, CA: Harper and Rowe Publishers, 1976), 41.

army. The Iraq war was promised to be short, too. In 2002, then Secretary of Defense Donald Rumsfeld said, "Five days or five months, but it certainly isn't going to last longer than that."

Like most of the young men of his generation Paul Tillich marched to war full of hope for a quick victory and the subsequent glories to follow. This was not to be. The German advance on Paris stalemated in France, and by the armistice in November 1918, Germany alone had lost three-quarter million men, suffered four million casualties, and experienced a national debt near forty-four billion dollars.[4] I don't know if this sounds familiar or not, at least the financial situation.

Chaplain Paul Tillich participated in three of the four major battles of World War I. He was at Verdun, the Somme, and the Marne. The Battle of the Somme was one of the most costly battles in the history of warfare.[5] In the first day of the five-month battle, 19,240 British soldiers were killed. When the battle ended, 300,000 British, Commonwealth, French, and German soldiers were killed and twice as many were wounded. During these battles, and the grueling monotony between them, Paul Tillich was a good chaplain. He quickly adapted to the rigors of living in the field and did everything he could to make life better for his soldiers and fellow staff officers. He held regular services in bombed out churches or in the trenches when the opportunity for a moment of peace presented itself. He rallied the troops with stirring sermons. In one such sermon he said, "Your heroism, your pain, my dear comrades, bear eternity in them. They have a brilliance and a glory which will light up when all earthly brilliance is sunk in dust and rot."[6] The small silver chalice that he carried is on display at the Harvard University Library.

When the brutal combat of trench warfare climaxed, Chaplain Tillich sprang into action. His first concern was the evacuation of the wounded and in doing this, he became like a madman, running into the fray and dragging wounded

---

[4] Ibid, 55.

[5] Martin Gilbert, *The Somme: Heroism and Horror in the First World War* (New York: Henry Holt and Company, 2006), xvii.

[6] Pauck, *Paul Tillich*, 46.

men to safety. For this he was awarded the Iron Cross First Class, the German equivalent to our Medal of Honor. But the carnage eventually took a toll on the young, academically minded pastor-turned combat chaplain. By the war's end he had buried thousands, many with his own hands in the mucky clay of war-torn France. When his friend Bartenstein was killed he could not speak at the burial, but only read from the service book. Three times after the intense rage of battle he collapsed where he stood and was evacuated to a hospital to recover. Many years later, first-hand accounts from his family and friends indicate he never fully healed from the psychological and spiritual wounds he received in World War I.[7] For the rest of his life, he would often awaken everyone in his apartment with screams, the result of his nightmarish memories of those days in combat. He wrote to his father that, "Body and soul are broken and can never be entirely repaired, but that is a small sacrifice in comparison with millions who have given their lives."[8]

You and I know I didn't experience anything close to the trenches of World War I. I was in Baghdad when the civil war started, but my war was different and I wasn't as traumatized as Tillich. I've only awakened my housemates screaming a few times, at least so far.

When the war was over Tillich returned to a devastated Germany. He also returned to a wife who was pregnant by another man. A quick divorce followed, and Tillich was able to legally declare in court that the child was not his. Tillich poured himself into academic pursuits and the wild, bohemian culture of postwar Berlin. His apartment was nicknamed the Katastrophen-Diele, the Disaster Bar. For the next five years this apartment witnessed an abortion, the birth of a baby, and a brutal robbery.[9] Soon the apartment became a haven for struggling artists and students. During this time he experienced a "multiplicity of erotic relationships" that left him with "manifold fears, expectations, ecstasies, and despairs."[10] It was a time of chaos when he was the "wild man."

---

[7] Arther, "Paul Tillich as a Military Chaplain," 1.

[8] Ibid, 54.

[9] German, "Katastrophen-Diele," Pauck, *Paul Tillich*, 79.

[10] Pauck, *Paul Tillich*, 82.

I came home to a similar situation. Although my wife was not pregnant, she eventually married the man with whom she had an affair. I plunged myself into my work as a hospital chaplain and moved into a small apartment in Washington, D.C. with several roommates. *Death Letter* is the account of my "multiplicity of erotic relationships" and my "manifold fears, expectations, ecstasies, and despairs."

Five years after the war he met Hannah Werner, ten years his junior, and married her. They had an open marriage—as the memoir that Hannah wrote after Paul's death made clear to the world.[11] His affairs outnumbered hers, and if it were not for moving to New York from Germany when Paul Tillich was forty-six, it is unlikely they would have stayed together. In spite of their struggles, all told in great detail in Hannah's From Time to Time, Hannah was at Paul's side when he died in Chicago in 1965.

I hope my healing journey will be more healing than Tillich's was. I've learned many things from his journey, and also see his life as a cautionary tale. I explored Paul Tillich's experience as an Army chaplain in World War I and his search for healing in my Doctor of Ministry dissertation. Tillich's search for healing, I believe, can be of help to military chaplains and warriors who experience a change in their relationship with God in war. I believe his theological insights are uniquely helpful to warriors with combat trauma because they come to us from a person who lost something of himself and even God in combat. Tillich's whole experience of WWI and his search for healing might be summed up in the final line of his most popular book, "The courage to be is rooted in the God who appears when God disappears in the anxiety of doubt."[12]

---

[11] Hannah Tillich, *From Time to Time* (New York: Stein and Day, 1974).

[12] Paul Tillich, *The Courage to Be*. 2nd Edition (New Haven, CT: Yale University Press, 2000) 49.

CREDITS AND CONTRIBUTORS

Publishing: Tactical 16, LLC
CEO, Tactical 16: Erik Shaw
President, Tactical 16: Jeremy Farnes
Cover Design: Bryan Dolch

ABOUT THE AUTHOR
David W. Peters

www.DavidWPeters.com

David W. Peters enlisted in the Marine Corps the day after his high school graduation. Ten years later, after the invasion of Iraq, he was commissioned as an Army Chaplain. Peters served as the battalion chaplain for the 62nd Engineer Combat Battalion (Heavy) at Fort Hood, Texas, from 2004 to 2007, which included his deployment to Baghdad, Iraq in 2006. After his return, he served as a chaplain clinician in the amputee, orthopedic, neuroscience, and psychological wards at Walter Reed Army Medical Center in Washington, D. C. He is a contributor to the *Huffington Post* and the Oxford University Press blog. His essay "A Spiritual War: Crises of Faith in Combat Chaplains from Iraq and Afghanistan," is included in *Listening on the Edge: Oral History in the Aftermath of Crisis* (Oxford University Press, 2014). His sermon, "Learning War and Reconciliation," won the national Reconciliation Preaching Prize from Trinity, Wall Street. On 9/11/2015, he preached it to first responders at Ground Zero in NYC. David works as a parish priest in The Episcopal Church and founded both the Episcopal Veterans Fellowship and the Hospitallers of St. Martin, a new monastic Christian Community for veterans ministry. He lives with his wife and children in Austin, Texas.

ABOUT THE PUBLISHER
Tactical 16, LLC

Tactical 16 is a Veteran owned and operated publishing company based in the beautiful mountain city of Colorado Springs, Colorado. What started as an idea among like-minded people has grown into reality.

Tactical 16 believes strongly in the healing power of writing, and provides opportunities for Veterans, Police, Firefighters, and EMTs to share their stories; striving to provide accessible and affordable publishing solutions that get the works of true American Heroes out to the world. We strive to make the writing and publication process as enjoyable and stress-free as possible.

As part of the process of healing and helping true American Heroes, we are honored to hear stories from all Veterans, Police Officers, Firefighters, EMTs and their spouses. Regardless of whether it's carrying a badge, fighting in a war zone or family at home keeping everything going, we know many have a story to tell.

At Tactical 16, we truly stand behind our mission to be "The Premier Publishing Resource for Guardians of Freedom."

We are a proud supporter of Our Country and its People, without which we would not be able to make Tactical 16 a reality.

How did Tactical 16 get its name? There are two parts to the name, "Tactical" and "16". Each has a different meaning. Tactical refers to the Armed Forces, Police, Fire, and Rescue communities or any group who loves, believes in, and supports Our Country. The "16" is the number of acres of the World Trade Center complex that was destroyed on that harrowing day of September 11, 2001. That day will be forever ingrained in the memories of many generations of Americans. But that day is also a reminder of the resolve of this Country's People and the courage, dedication, honor, and integrity of our Armed Forces, Police, Fire, and Rescue communities. Without Americans willing to risk their lives to defend and protect Our Country, we would not have the opportunities we have before us today.

More works from Tactical 16 available at www.tactical16.com.

Safe From the War
By: Chris Hernandez

Line in the Valley
By: Chris Hernandez

Proof of Our Resolve
By: Chris Hernandez

**What They Don't Teach You
in Deer River**
By: Julia A. Maki

Death Letter
By: David W. Peters

The Pact
By: Robert Patrick Lewis

Love Me When I'm Gone
*The True Story of Life, Love, and Loss
for a Green Beret in Post-9/11 War*
By: Robert Patrick Lewis

And Then I Cried:
Stories of a Mortuary NCO
By: Robert Patrick Lewis

Ashley's High Five for Daddy
By: Pam Saulsby

Losing the War in Vietnam
*But Winning the War to Reclaim
My Soul*
By: Frank DiScala

Zuzu's Petals
By: Kevin Andrew

Thank you to the following sponsor for supporting this project:

Steel City Vets

Pittsburgh, Pennsylvania

Steel City Vets, Pittsburgh's first Post 9/11 Veterans support organization focusing on connecting Veterans, serves the over 50,000 Veterans of Afghanistan and Iraq that reside in the Greater Pittsburgh and South Western PA region. Through social activites, SCV aims to be a resource for Veterans through their transition from the military to civilian life.

Steel City Vets is a Veteran founded and run non-profit. For more information please visit their website at **steelcityvets.org** and connect with them on Facebook by visiting **facebook.com/steelcityvets**.

Printed in the USA
CPSIA information can be obtained
at www.ICGtesting.com
JSHW010800140923
48136JS00012B/88